GARY JONES

Travel

London,Paris,Amsterdam,Edinburgh

Contents

1

LONDON - INTRODUCTION

This guide was designed for people with limited time in London and who want to get the most out of their short stay.This is not a long book about everything in London.This book is the London essentials.

London is an amazing city and has a rich history that stretches back for two millennia.Today London is a trend-setting global city and have great experiences to offer visitors.London is a city of diversities, old mixed with new.On London streets, you will find people from all over the world that live and work in London.It's a true global city.

If you have limited time in London, then my advice to you is not to try and see everything.Rather go to the best London has to offer and leave the rest for another trip.London will be a great experience if you take your time and truly experience the best the city has to offer.Don't spend 5 minutes in every attraction in London and never really experience the energy of London.

This book will give you a good glimpse and idea of what London has to offer.

Despite all the landmarks, structures and testament to its ancient roots, London is a highly urban place, dotted with history. From the Tower of London and similar buildings to the modern clubs and restaurants, experience the mingling of the ancient and the modern, all in one harmonious symphony.

I wrote this book with a limited time frame in mind.Go see the best of London and spend some quality time there.This way you will really experience this amazing city and have memories you can carry with you forever.

I hope you have a great time in London!

Good Luck!

2

Crash Course on the History of London

London is the place where history was made. It has witnessed the rise and fall of empires, families, leaders, tyrants, and politicians. It also became home to artists and scientists alike. With its long history, London might just have seen it all.

The city's name originated from a Celtic word- Londinios- meaning "where the bold one is". In 43 AD, the Romans invaded Britain and then built a bridge across the River Thames. Later, the Romans realized the attractive possibility of building a port in the place. It was perfectly situated; it was far away inland from Germanic raiders, but the water was still deep enough for large ships to come in.

London quickly became the largest British town. It became a typical Roman city, with a forum in the center, amphitheaters and numerous bathhouses.

During the Dark Ages, London ceased to be a town. The walls were still intact, but only a few people lived within the town. After a few years, it rose from obscurity. The new town was much smaller. The town soon became a bustling location where ships from all over Europe landed. By the early 8th century, London became a trading center.

The Danes looted London in 842, and later conquered the rest of Northern and Eastern parts of England. In 878, King Alfred the Great defeated the invading Danes. England was divided, and London remained under the Danes. King Alfred took London back in 886 and repaired the old Roman walls. The entire town returned to its original state and became a flourishing town once more.

London Bridge is falling down...

The popular children's rhyme is believed to be a historical fact. It was believed to happen in the early parts of the 11th century. The king of Norway, King Olaf, attacked England. His men found it difficult to sail up the River Thames and past the London Bridge. King Olaf had his men sail to the London Bridge, the boats protected by wicker and wood canopies.

Once the boats were under the bridge, the men sailed close to the bridge's wooden struts and tied ropes around them. They rowed the boats away from the bridge, pulling the supporting struts, which caused the bridge to collapse.

London during the Middle Ages

During the Middle Ages, some of the most famous London structures were built. In 1066, London had a charter that confirmed certain rights to its town and citizens. The charter was given by William the Conqueror. From 1078 to 1100, a stone tower was built to replace the wooden one built by William, which stood guard over the town of London. This stone tower was the ancestor of what would later become the infamous Tower of London.

A stone bridge was built in 1176. This replaced the older wooden one that spanned the Thames River. In 1180, London was described as a happy, thriving town, with clean air. The people enjoyed religious contentment, with strong fortifications that protected them.

London during the 16th and 17th Century

Prosperity continued during these periods. More lands opened up for new buildings and new suburban areas that accommodated the increasing London population. London continued to expand until in 1600, the town is connected to the Westminster Palace through a row of houses.

In 1622, the Banqueting House was built. Hyde Park was opened to the public by the king in 1635. Richmond Park was created in 1637, which served as a hunting ground for Charles I and his court. Greenwich, which was near the flourishing London town, became the site for the building of the Queen's House in 1637.

In 1571, the Royal Exchange opened. It catered to the growing and bustling trade. Wool was London's main export. There were also several other trade goods such as rabbits' and sheep' skins, tin, lead and a myriad of spices and herbs.

The growth and progress of London continued despite the bubonic plague. Outbreaks occurred in 1603, and again in 1633 and 1665. After each outbreak, London's population was able to quickly recover.

During the rest of the 17th century, several civil wars and rebellions occurred. Then, in 1666, the great London fire occurred. The fire started small in a baker's house located in Pudding Lane, but because of the wind, it soon spread. It destroyed about 13,200 houses, leaving about 70,000 to 80,000 people homeless. Because of this disaster, the king ordered that all houses built in London should be made of brick and stone. St. Paul's was also a casualty of this fire. Rebuilding efforts started in 1675 and was finished in 1711.

London during the 18th century

Rapid population growth happened from the late 17th century to the 18th century. Hospitals were built during this period, such as Westminster in 1720, Guys in 1724, St Georges in 1733, London in 1740 and Middlesex in 1745.

In 1703, the famous Buckingham Palace was constructed for the equally famous Duke of Buckingham. John Nash altered the palace in the 10th century. In 1837, the first monarch to ever live in this palace was Queen Victoria.

Other notable establishments built during this period were:
- Marlborough House in 1711
- British Museum in 1753
- Mansion House in 175e, built to serve as the Lord Mayor of London's residence
- Houses built on the London Bridge were demolished in 1757
- Walls surrounding the city were demolished in 1760 to 1766
- New bridge built in Westminster in 1749
- Blackfriar's bridge built in 1770
- Somerset House built by Sir William Chambers in 1176–1786

London during the 19th century

The main activity in London during this time is expansion. One of the major reasons for this growth was the establishment of the railway system. In 1837, Euston Station was established. In 1852, the famous Kings Cross Station was constructed. The St Pancras' Station was constructed in 1868.

Other notable events in the 19th century were:
- In 1863, London witnessed the opening of the 1st underground railway system. Steam trains pulled the 1st carriages
- Train system ran on electricity, started on 1890 and became fully electric in 1905
- Thames Tunnel was constructed in 1843.
- Parliament burned down in 1834, which Charles Barry rebuilt and included the now famous Big Ben clock tower.
- Trafalgar Square was created in 1839, with the Nelsons column built in 1842.
- Regents Park was opened to the public in 1838.
- Victoria Park was opened to the public in 1845
- Battersea Park was opened in 1858.
- Albert Hall, one of London's great landmarks was constructed in 1871.
- Museums opened such as Victoria & Albert Museum (more popularly referred to as the V & A) in 1852, Science Museum in 1857 and Natural History Museum in 1881.
- In 1891, The New Scotland Yard was constructed.
- In 1892, Piccadilly Square's statue of Eros was built

London during the 20th century

Early 20th century saw the continuation of progress in

London. More structures were built such as:

- Westminster Cathedral in 1903
- V & A Museum moved in 1909 to where it is located today
- Geological Museum in 1935
- White City Stadium in 1908
- Wembley Stadium in 1923
- Gunnersbury Park in 1925
- Chiswick Bridge in 1933

Progress halted in World War II. London experienced huge losses. In September 1940, the Blitz began and more and more Londoners started sleeping in the city's underground stations. About 20,000 people died, and 25,000 were injured during this period.

After the war, London slowly got back to its feet. The city reconstructed what the war damaged. It even built some more:

- In 1945, the Waterloo Bridge was constructed.
- In 1951, the Royal Festival Hall was constructed.
- In 1956, the opening of the Pollock's Toy Museum took place.
- In 1962, the Shell Center opened.
- In 1963, the Millbank Tower was erected.
- In 1966, the Post Office Tower was opened, which quickly became one of the famous London landmarks.
- In 1968, opening of the Hayward's Gallery
- In 1976, opening of the Museum of London
- In 1979, opening of the Museum of Garden History
- In 1980, opening of the London Transport Museum
- In 1988, opening of the Museum of the Moving Image
- In 2000, the Somerset House was opened to the public.

London during the 21st century

London's growth continued rapidly at the start of the 21st century. There were many more sights and landmarks constructed and opened to the public:

- In 2000, the London Eye was opened to the public.
- In 2012, the Shard was opened.
- In 2012, Olympics was held in London, which confirmed its status as one of the greatest cities in the world.

Today, London's population is around 8.1 million. Many industries were founded and flourished in London, but the greatest as of today is tourism. Each year, millions of tourists come to the city to experience its long-standing history. The city's greatest attractions are the many landmarks and structures that were constructed over the centuries.

3

Transport

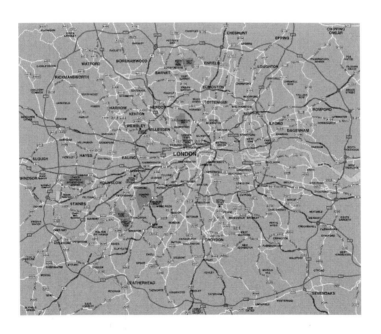

There are several ways to get from Heathrow Airport to London.If you are looking for a fast and easy way, then I recommend taking the Heathrow Express.It will take about 15 minutes from Heathrow to Paddington station.At Paddington Station, you can take the subway or taxi.(The Subway is called the Tube or Underground in London).The Heathrow Express runs every 15 minutes.

Heathrow Express Website

Phone: +44 (0) 345 600 1515

Heathrow Website

Heathrow Map

If you are looking for a cheap way from Heathrow, then take the subway from the airport.The subway trip will take about 1 hour to central London.

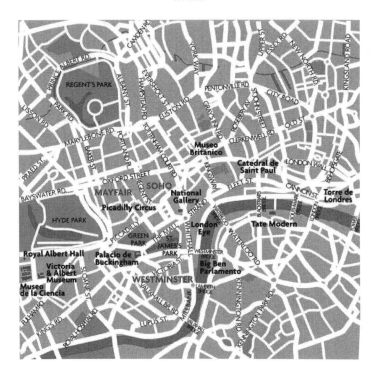

Subway(Underground or Tube)

Once in London the City subway system is very efficient and runs all over the city.To make your journey in London as convenient as possible buy an Oyster card.An Oyster card is an electronic card you can load up with cash or load with a weekly ticket.To make your transport in the city cheap and easy, I suggest you get a weekly ticket loaded up on your Oyster card.You can choose which Zones on the London underground you want your ticket to cover.The more Zones you cover, the more expensive.

London Underground Website

Phone:0343 222 1234

Buses

The London bus system can take you all over the city and easy to navigate.You can use your Oyster card to travel on all the city buses.

There are night buses that run after the subway closes that can take you back to the area you came from.

Taxis

If you want to take a taxi, then I suggest taking the traditional London black cabs.They all have the same unusual shape and can take up to 6 passengers.Inside you will notice the taxi driver ID and taxi number.

These taxis are safe and reliable.There is a cheaper option like minicabs, but they are not always reliable and not always safe especially when you travel alone, and it's late at night.The city regulates the traditional black cabs.The minicabs are just normal looking cars and sometimes have no recognizable sign that it's a taxi.

Taxis

Phone : 0871 871 8710

Thames River Bus

The Thames river bus is a great way to get around the city and see the amazing London attractions.These boats are faster than the normal river tour boats and will get you around the city fast.Refreshments and Wi-Fi are available on the boat.Tickets can be purchased at the pier ticket office.

Thames River Bus Website

Phone:020 7001 2200

4

Hotels

London is one of the most expensive cities in the world.So finding a good affordable hotel for your stay could be tricky, but I made a short list of some the best budget hotels in London.

Gloucester Place Hotel

Marylebone is one of the best areas in London, and you will be extremely central and walking distance to Oxford Street and Hyde Park.The hotel has traditional Georgian Style, and you will enjoy a very nice breakfast.The location is fantastic, and you can walk to Marble Arch Tube Station(subway) and Bond Street Tube Station.The legendary Madame Tussaud Museum is a 10-minute walk, and so is the Sherlock Holmes Museum in Baker Street.

Address: Gloucester Place Hotel, 55 -53 Gloucester Place, Near Harley Street, London W1U 6AT

Phone: 020 7486 6166

Gloucester Place Hotel Website

Central Park Hotel

This is one of the best areas in South West London and is a nice hideaway from all the tourist spots.The hotel is close to Queensway Underground Station.The location is amazing,its close to both Hyde Park and Oxford Street.

Address: 49 Queensborough Terrace, Westminster Borough,

Phone: 020 7229 2424

Central Park Hotel Website

Jesmond Hotel

The Jesmond Hotel is located in Bloomsbury and is also has the classic Georgian style.The hotel is close to Goodge Street Tube Station.One of the best things of this hotel is the lovely garden in the back where you can relax after a long day in the city.

Address: 63 Gower St, London WC1E 6HJ

Phone: 020 7636 3199

Jesmond Hotel Website

Point A Hotel London

If you don't really care about staying in a traditional English Hotel, and you would rather stay in a simple modern bed and breakfast with no thrills, then book a room at the Point A Hotel London.The Point A Hotel London is in the Paddington area so you can take the Heathrow Express train straight to Paddington and get in and out of London in a very convenient way.

Address:41 Praed St, London W2 1NR

Phone: 020 7258 3140

Point A Hotel London Website

5

London's Best Museums

What better way to see London's history and get a glimpse of its culture than by going to museums. There are numerous museums in and around the city. The best part about these museums, aside from their easy accessibility and wealth of history, is that most of them have free admissions.

The British Museum

This is London's, and among the world's, oldest museums. Located at 44 Great Russell Street, admission is free. Sometimes, there are admission charges for some of their temporary exhibitions.

The British Museum contains millions of objects. The collection is so vast that they can only be placed on display in batches. Tourists often make a beeline for certain popular exhibits like the Rosetta Stone, Lewis Chessmen, collection of mummies, the Sutton Hoo ship burial, and the Lindow Man.

The Sutton Hoo ship burial is the centerpiece of the recently opened Sir Paul and Lady Jill Ruddock Gallery. The display includes different finds across Europe, which dates back as early as AD 300 to 1100. In this exhibit, one can see the iconic Sutton Hoo masked helmet of the Anglo-Saxons. There are also mosaics that date back to the late Roman era.

Some of the many amazing objects include the Lycurgus Cup (dating back to the 4th century, which was extraordinarily designed to change its colors when exposed to different lights) and the remarkable Kells Crozier (9th century holy staff made from yew wood, decorated and modified through the years).

There are also some permanent exhibitions like:
- Enlightenment: Exhibit that covers the 18th century. It also showcases thousands of objects, some of which from the mid-18th century to the early parts of the 19th century. There is also the former King's Library, which was recently restored. It contained George III's book collection.
- Living & Dying: Permanent in the Wellcome Trust Gallery. The exhibit explores the different diseases diagnosed and treated throughout the course of history. It also dealt with how people across the centuries coped with death, including the different rituals on mourning, festivals for the dead and burial.

Address: Great Russell St, London WC1B 3DG
 Phone: 020 7323 8299
 British Museum Website

 British Museum Map

The V & A (Victoria and Albert Museum)

This is another of London's most notable museums that visitors must see. It is located in Knightsbridge and admission is free. The V & A is among the most magnificent museums in the entire world. The foundation stone of the museum was laid by Queen Victoria herself in 1899, which was also her last official engagement in public.

The museum has a marvelous display of applied arts coming from all over the world. There are 150 grand galleries within its 7 floors. There are countless objects including various furniture, sculptures, ceramics, paintings, jewelry, glass, metalwork, dress, textiles and posters. All these are from various centuries. Most notable objects are:

· Raphael cartoons (7 in all), which were created in 1515.

These were tapestry designs painted for the Sistine Chapel.
- A collection of sculptures during the Italian Renaissance, which are the most excellent in the category.
- Ardabil carpet, which is the oldest in the world and the most magnificent floor covering of all
- Jameel Gallery of Islamic Art
- Luck of Edenhall, which comes from Syria and is a 13th-century glass beaker
- Fashion galleries that showcase dresses ranging from 18th-century court dresses to contemporary chiffon ensemble
- Photography collection, famous for its more than 500,000 images
- Architecture Gallery, which houses numerous models, plans, descriptions and videos of various techniques

Address: Cromwell Rd, London SW7 2RL
  Phone:020 7942 2000
  The V & A Website

  The V & A Map

The Natural History Museum

This famous museum is located along Gloucester Road. Admission is free. This astounding museum doubles as a research institution. The Natural History Museum opened in 1881, in the purpose built Palazzo of Alfred Waterhouse, which is in the Romanesque style. The NHM is now joined by the extension of the magnificent Darwin Center. The façade is in a magnificent pale blue and terracotta design.

Visitors are greeted by a Diplodocus skeleton, which takes up the entire length of the huge entrance hall. Going deeper inside the building will reveal the wonderful and exotic world of different creatures that roamed the earth then and now.

Address: Cromwell Rd, London SW7 5BD

Phone:020 7942 5000

Natural History Museum Website

Natural History Museum Map

The Science Museum

The Science Museum is in Knightsbridge and visitors are admitted for free. The museum has 7 floors that contain a wealth of entertaining and educational exhibits. One of the most notable exhibits is the command module of the famous Apollo 11. There is also a flight simulator in the museum's exhibit. Other notable exhibits include:

- Wellcome Wing (developments in contemporary medicine, science, and technology)
- Medical History Gallery (collection of treasures in medical history)
- Pattern Pod (importance of patterns in modern-day science)
- Launch Pad (hands-on gallery that allows children to explore the basic principles of science)

Address: Exhibition Rd, London SW7 2DD
  Phone:0870 870 4868
  Science Museum Website

  Science Museum Map

Leighton House Museum

Similar to the Charles Dickens Museum, the Leighton House Museum was once the former home of Victorian artist Lord Frederic Leighton (1830 - 1896). It is a very fancy and remarkable infrastructure that was built during the 19th century. This house contains numerous paintings and sculptures that were crafted by Lord Leighton and his colleagues.

Leighton's place started out as a small house. But as he gained popularity, he embellished and extended his abode and turned it into a majestic palace of art. It boasts of the splendid Arab Hall, where your eyes will feast on a golden dome, elaborate mosaics, and walls that are lined with gorgeous Islamic tiles.

Lord's Leighton's vast painting studio, which is located on the upper floor, is one of the must-see sights for art lovers who are visiting London. It is filled with numerous paintings that are in their different stages of completion, and the walls are lined with his masterpieces. Popular figures from the Victorian age were given the chance to peruse inside the famous room. Queen Victoria, for instance, walked around these halls in 1859. The Leighton House Museum has different kinds of paintings in their collection.

They have 76 oil paintings that consist of the small, loosely-painted color sketches that Lord Leighton created as part of his picture-making process. Larger scale versions of these oil paintings can be found in the exhibition at the Royal Academy.

When it comes to sculpture, the famous artist has created three masterpieces. They may be few, but their influence over the new generation of British sculptors was massive in scale. The museum holds the three sculptures, which are – An Athlete Wrestling with a Python, The Sluggard, and Needless Alarms. The exhibit also has the plaster casts of the first sketch design for An Athlete Wrestling with a Python.

The biggest collection of this museum is Lord Leighton's

drawings that are composed of 700 pieces of his sketches and studies. This collection was created to show his talent and skill as a draughtsman. The collection includes sketches from his younger years up to the time of his death.

Address: 12 Holland Park Rd, London W14 8LZ
Phone:+44 20 7602 3316
Leighton House Museum Website

Leighton House Museum Map

Charles Dickens Museum

At some point in our childhood, the famous author Charles Dickens has touched our lives with his beautiful literary masterpieces such as Oliver Twist, David Copperfield, Pickwick Papers, and A Tale of Two Cities. Now, you can relive the fun experience again and learn more about this great author at the Charles Dickens Museum.

This museum is located at 48 Doughty Street in the heart of Bloomsbury. This is also Charles Dicken's only surviving house in London. It was here where he finished Oliver Twist and started writing Nicholas Nickleby.

Visiting this house will provide you with a once in a lifetime opportunity to discover what would have been like when he was still living here, and learn more about his life and works.

Wandering through the rooms is like seeing how life and literature intertwine in perfect harmony. The author's old drawing room is filled with paintings, prints, and his reading desk, which gave birth to various beloved fictional characters.

The attic, on the other hand, shows the author's upheavals during his younger years and portrays them using several displays. There is a barred window from Marshalsea debtor's prison – the home of his family for years.

The entire museum holds 100,000 different other items including old manuscripts from his previous works, special editions, and some of his personal items. Each artifact is well preserved to maintain their beauty over the years.
In the house next door, there is a café where you can rest and have a little chat with fellow literary enthusiasts while sipping a cup of tea.

If you need to hold an event, the Charles Dickens Museum will be much happy to accommodate your needs. You can reserve some of its rooms when you want to conduct launch parties or business conferences. They have a very atmospheric and light environment that is ideal for a wide range of events.
Address: 48 Doughty St, London WC1N 2LX
Phone:020 7405 2127
Charles Dickens Museum Website

Charles Dickens Museum Map

Grant Museum of Zoology
Aside from high fashion, art, and music, the United Kingdom is also well-known for its breakthroughs in scientific

discoveries. The Grant Museum Zoology is the only remaining zoological museum in London. It boasts of a collection of more than 67,000 specimens that were collected from various species in the animal kingdom.

The museum was established in 1828 by Robert Edmond Grant. It was first used as a teaching collection for the University of London (now called University College London) which was also newly built at that time. In its 180 years of its existence, it has survived wars, flooding, and threats of closure.

The Grant Museum of Zoology is also considered as a "museum within a museum" because numerous collections from other local universities were transported here when they closed.

In here, you can see a collection of animal brains finely preserved in chemical fluids, collected specimens from expeditions such as Discovery, Challenger, and the Great Barrier Reef. There are also fossils of hominid materials, and also specimens of extinct or endangered animals like the Tasmanian Tiger, Quagga, giant deers, and the Dodo bird.

Aside from being a tourist attraction, this museum is also a great hub for knowledge. Researchers and scientists are warmly welcome to study here and peruse the full collection of the museum's specimens. Their collection includes a wide array of materials like fluid preserved species, pinned entomology, taxidermy, freeze-dried, and skeletal specimens.

Oftentimes, they also held special events in the museum. They will feature seminars, film showings, and even games or competitions. Most of these are free.

The Grant Museum of Zoology is open to the public every Monday to Saturday between 1 to 5 pm. If you want to conduct group and research visits, they are also open during the weekdays from 10 am to 1 pm. However, make sure that you book your reservations in advance.

Address:21 University St, London WC1E 6DE

Phone:020 3108 2052

Grant Museum of Zoology Website

Grant Museum of Zoology Map

The National Maritime Museum

The National Maritime Museum in London is the largest Maritime Museum in the world.In this museum, you will experience the incredible stories of maritime exploration around the world.A visit to this museum is a remarkable experience.

The museum is located in Greenwich one of London's most historic areas.The museum is open daily 10am-5pm.Take a train Greenwich Station to get there.
Address:Park Row, Greenwich, London SE10 9NF
Phone:020 8858 4422
The National Maritime Museum Website

The National Maritime Museum Map

The Household Cavalry Museum
This military museum is unique in the sense that it will give you a behind the scenes look at the life of the Household Cavalry Regiment of the British Army.Visitors can take an inside look at the working stables of The Queen's Life Guard.The days to day life of the soldiers can be observed here.The tradition of the Queens Gaurd dates back 350 years. .To get there by subway go to Charing Cross station.The Museum is located in Whitehall and is a few minutes away from the subway station.

Address:The Household Division, Horse Guards,
   Whitehall, London SW1A 2AX
   Phone:020 7930 3070
   Household Cavalry Museum Website

   Household Cavalry Museum Map

6

Art in London

London, over the centuries, has been home to various artists. It has always supported grandmasters of the arts, as well as the obscure ones. Today, numerous art galleries pepper the city, exhibiting various art pieces from all over the world. The exhibits range from the classic to modern art.

Tate Modern

Admission is free in Tate Modern. This is among the top-ranking art galleries located in London. Tate Modern is considered in the art-world as a powerhouse for the modern art. The building is done in industrial architectural style. After all, the building was originally built as a power station after the Second World War. Sir Giles Gilbert Scott designed the original building, which was shut down in 1981.

Almost 20 years later, the former power station became a powerhouse that catered to modern art. Every year, about 5 million visitors marvel at the exhibits in Tate Modern. This huge visitor traffic prompted the highly ambitious expansion in 2012, which was called the Tanks. The name was in reference to the use of immensely cavernous old oil tanks. The Tanks is meant to hold film art and stage performances.

Large-scale installations are temporarily on display in the turbine hall, which is effective in lending awesome effects to the installations. There are also the permanent collections that consist of international modern art works from 1900 to present. The main galleries also permanently feature the works of the greats such as Beuys, Matisse and Rothko. All the artworks are expertly curated and grouped according to movement such as Post-war abstraction, Minimalist, Surrealism, etc.

Address:Bankside, London SE1 9TG
Phone:020 7887 8888
Tate Modern Website

Tate Modern Map

The National Gallery

Located at the equally stunning Trafalgar Square, the National Museum is one of London's must-see art galleries. The gallery's collection of European paintings number to more than 2,000, ranging from works done from the Middle Ages up to the 20th century. Inspiring and awesome works of the masters like Leonardo da Vinci, Renoir, Van Gogh, Gainsborough, Rembrandt and Turner. Practically, all European schools of art are represented in the National Gallery's collection.

The gallery is divided in several exhibits housed in wings:
- Sainsbury Wing extension: earliest art works that the gallery owned like Italian paintings made by the early masters such as Piero Della Francesca and Giotto
- Sainsbury Wing basement: for temporary exhibitions
- West Wing: Italian Renaissance by Raphael, Titian, and

Correggio
- North Wing: works by 17th century Italian, Flemish, Spanish and Dutch Old Masters
- East Wing: most popular paintings done by French Impressionists and post-Impressionists, such as the famous water lily paintings of Claude Monet and the sunflower series of Vincent Van Gogh

Address: Trafalgar Square, London WC2N 5DN
Phone:020 7747 2885
The National Gallery Website

The National Gallery Map

The ICA
The Institute of Contemporary Arts was originally founded to steer the art scene of the city towards a bolder and more daring new territory. This art gallery was a result of the collective efforts of various critics, artists, and poets in 1947. Most of the works here veer away from the laid-back themes of other schools of art. The collection is more on the rebellious kind of art.

Aside from the collections, the ICA also features cutting-edge bands, performance art, arthouse cinema performances, art-themed club nights and philosophical debates, among a few others that are meant to challenge accepted notions.

Address: The Mall, London SW1Y 5AH
Phone:020 7930 3647
The ICA Website

The ICA Map

The Barbican

This Barbican is a performing arts center and is one of the largest in Europe.The gallery hosts many art exhibitions and classical music concerts.The London Symphony Orchestra and the BBC Symphony Orchestra are based in this gallery.To get to the Barbican by subway go to Barbican subway station.

Address: Silk St, London EC2Y 8DS
Phone:020 7638 4141
The Barbican Map

Somerset House

Somerset House has a collection of old masters and Impressionist and Post-impressionist paintings.This classical building that was constructed in 1776 hosts many rotating exhibitions that focus on art, design, fashion, and photography.To get there take the subway to Temple or Covent Garden stations.

Address: Strand, London WC2R 1LA
  Phone:020 7845 4600
  Somerset House Website

  Somerset House Map

The Royal Academy of Arts

The Royal Academy of Arts is is the oldest fine arts institution in Britain.The Academy is based in based in Burlington House on Piccadilly and was founded in 1768.The academy is special in the sense that it is an independent, privately funded institution led by eminent artists and architects.This unique situation gives it total artistic freedom.The Academy hosts some of the best temporary and touring exhibitions.To get

43

there by subway go to Piccadilly Circus station.

Address: Burlington House, Piccadilly, London W1J 0BD
Phone:020 7300 8090
The Royal Academy of Arts Website

The Royal Academy of Arts Map

7

Historical Places

Buckingham Palace

A tour around London is not complete without stopping by at the Buckingham Palace. This tourist destination serves as a workplace and official London residence of the monarchy of the United Kingdom. This is one of the very few working royal palaces in the world. It is located in the City of Westminster.

The Buckingham Palace is mainly used by the Queen for official events and receptions. However, its State Rooms are open for public viewing every year. This grand palace is composed of 775 rooms. It has 19 State rooms, 52 Royal and guest bedrooms, 188 staff bedrooms, 92 offices, and 78 bathrooms.

The infrastructure measures 108 meters long across the front, 120 meters deep, and has a height of 24 meters.

This palace is furnished with numerous works of art that forms the Royal Collection, one of the largest art collections in the world, even though it is not an art gallery or a museum. These include work from Rembrandt, Rubens, and Canaletto.

Tourists who are planning to visit the Buckingham Palace will have a splendid time entering inside its grand halls. One of the most highly-recommended places to visit is the Windsor Castle, which houses the Great Kitchen. This is the oldest and the most substantially unchanged working kitchens in the country and has remained busy for 750 years.

The State Rooms, on the other hand, will show you a glimpse of the monarchy's history through art. Its gilded ceilings and glittering chandeliers make it a befitting location to place some of the Royal Collection's fine masterpieces.

In addition, you can also take a leisurely stroll in the palace garden. The best places to visit is the Herbaceous Border, the wisteria-clad summer house, the rose garden, and the Palace tennis court where King George VI and Fred Perry had a friendly match in the 1930s.

Address: London SW1A 1AA
Phone:0303 123 7300
Buckingham Palace Website

Buckingham Palace Map

Tower of London

The colossal infrastructure that is the Tower of London is a prime example of Norman military architecture. Built by William the Conqueror on the Thames, this tower is created to protect London and ensure that his power will stay intact. It has a very rich layer of history and is considered as one of the most significant symbols of royalty.

There are various places and artifacts to visit in the Tower of London. The infrastructure is the keeper of the famous Crown Jewels. You will be able to see numerous artifacts that British monarchs have used over centuries such as the coronation spoon, sovereign's scepter with cross, St. Edward's crown, the imperial state crown, and the crown of Queen Elizabeth.

Another spectacle to view in the Tower of London is the Yeomen warders. Popularly known as the Beefeaters, they have been guarding the tower for centuries and their origins stretch back as far as Edward IV's reign. You can talk to modern day Yeomen warders and discover tales about intrigue, torture, execution, and a whole lot more.

Other activities that you can try are spotting the legendary ravens around the tower, seeing the terrifying instruments of torture in the Wakefield Tower, and the Fusilier Museum.

Address:London EC3N 4AB
Phone:0844 482 7777
Tower of London Website

Tower of London Map

Extra Time
St Paul's Cathedral

St Paul's Cathedral is one of the most famous landmarks in London.The original church that was built on the same site dates back to 604AD.The current structure was built and finished in 1708.This Anglican Cathedral is the second biggest in England.

Address:St. Paul's Churchyard, London EC4M 8AD
Phone:020 7246 8350
St Paul's Cathedral Website

St Paul's Cathedral Map

Westminster Abbey

The spectacular church is a massive gothic style abbey chuch.This church plays a important part in the history of England and the United Kingdom. Westminster Abbey is the traditional place of coronation and is also the burial site for English and, later, British royalty.

Address:20 Deans Yd, London SW1P 3PA
    Phone:020 7222 5152
    Westminster Abbey Website

    Westminster Abbey Map

Houses of Parliament

The Palace of Westminster is also known as the Houses of
Parliament and is the meeting place for the House of Commons
and the House of Lords.The drama of British Politics happens
between these walls.The Palace of Westminster was the main
residence of the Kings of England until a fire destroyed much
of the building in 1512.

Address:London SW1A 0AA
Phone:020 7219 3000
Houses of Parliament Website

Houses of Parliament Map

Kensington Palace

Kensington Palace is most famous for being the official residence of Princess Diana.It remained the official residence of the Princess after her divorce until her death. Kensington Palace has been an official residence of the British Royal Family since the 17th century.

Address:Kensington Gardens, London W8 4PX
   Phone:020 3166 6000
   Kensington Palace Website

   Kensington Palace Map

8

Cosmopolitan London

London is a very cosmopolitan city and its a melting pot of cultures and nationalities.Let's take a look at a few interesting places in London.

Chinatown

If you wanted to visit a place where the oriental and western cultures blend together in harmony, then London's Chinatown is the best place for you.

The Chinese community of businesses and restaurants in London had a very long history dating back in the 18th century. The community started out in the city's East End side. The community's popularity bloomed in the 1950s, when British soldiers who came from the Far East discovered the rich and savory flavors of the Chinese cuisine. In the present times, the Chinese community has grown larger than before and is now located in the west of the Charring Cross road and is greatly concentrated on Gerard Street and Lisle Street.

If you are in Chinatown, one of the first things that should do is to fill your tummies with the most delicious oriental dishes. There's the Baozi Inn that offers spicy delicacies that are cheap yet flavorful, the Café TPT that boasts a wide menu of Hong Kong inspired dishes and good service, or the Four Seasons restaurant, which is popular for their Cantonese-style roast duck. Whether you are looking for cheap meals or high-end restaurants, there is always a place in Chinatown that fits your budget.

In addition, you can also improve your cooking skills by trying to whip up your own Chinese dish. The New Loon Fung market is a large hive that sells oriental produce such as chrysanthemum tea, ginger, and spinach noodles.

Chinatown is best visited during January to February where the community celebrates the Chinese New Year. The dragon dances and the fireworks display are truly a sight to behold.

Address:55-57 Charing Cross Rd, London WC2H 0BL
Phone:020 7287 2220
Chinatown Website

China Town Map

Camden Town

Camden is another interesting area of London is seen as the main area of alternative culture in London.Walking down the streets of Camden will bring you into a mix of markets and music venues.

Camden is famous for arts, music and just being different.Camden is symbol of the cosmopolitan nature od London and is a melting pot of different elements in London finding expression through art and music.

Getting to Camden is easy with Camden Town subway station being close to all the markets and main attractions in the area.

The Camden Markets is something special and offers a wide variety of fashion, food , books and antiques.If you are looking for alternative goods then Camden is the place for you.

Camden Town Website

Camden Town Map

Edgware Road

The Southern part of Edgware Road is well known for its diverse Middleastern and African cultural influence.If you love Middle Eastern Food then Edgware Road is the place for you.Late at night you will find

many 24-hour kebab and shawarma restaurants.

To get to Edgware Road by subway ,get off at the Edgware Road station.

Edgware Road Map

9

Shopping

London is also the home of street fashion and couture thriving well side-by-side. Even the small street shops offer some incredible finds. The best shopping districts for different tastes include this short list:

Oxford Street

This is heart of the shopping experience in the city of London. Here, shoppers are greeted with over 300 different shops, including landmark stores and designer outlets. This is also where the renowned Selfridges is found.

All of the famous high end chains have their shops in Oxford Street, along with famous department store chains Debenhams and John Lewis. While in Oxford, one can easily slip into a side street to get out of the opulent shopping experience and into Berwick Street and St Christopher's Place among others for a few real treats.

Oxford Street Website

Oxford Street Map

Mayfair and Bond Street

This is where you can find people who wish to burn money, splurge on some high quality designer clothes or feast the eyes on luxurious items. This is also considered as London's exclusive shopping area where the rich and the celebrities go on shopping sprees. Shops include Tiffany & Co., Louis Vuitton and Burberry.

Mayfair Map

Carnaby Street

This is an iconic shopping district just 2 minutes away from the Piccadilly Circus and Oxford Circus. Carnaby Street gave birth to the cultural and fashion revolution in the 60s. The iconic arch is a gateway to some historic shopping experience. Over 150 brands and more than 50 independent bars and restaurants can be found along this historic street. It also hosts a fascinating mix of heritage brands, stores, new designer names and independent boutiques.

Carnaby Street Website

Carnaby Street Map

Covent Garden

This is the place to go for those who are looking for unique items, hip fashion, handmade one-of-a-kind jewelry or rare sweets. Neal Street offers funky cosmetics, latest urban streetwear and some funky unique shoes. Covent Garden Market is where interesting arts and crafts are found. Distinctive London shopping experience can also be experienced along St Martin's Courtyard, Seven Dials, Shorts Gardens, Neal's Yard, Monmouth Street and Floral Street.

Covent Garden Website

Covent Garden Map

King's Road

Shopping is the main obsession in this place. Shoppers are treated to unique labels, high-street labels, designer shops and trendy boutiques. Vivienne Westwood's Shop is found here, which gave birth to punk fashion in the 70s.

King's Road Map

Knight's Bridge

Knightsbridge and Brompton Road is the go-to place of visitors all over the world looking to shop illustrious brands. Harvey Nichols and Harrods are located here, along with other shops that offer the latest trends.

Knight's Bridge Map

Notting Hill

This was made famous by a Hollywood movie of the same name. Quite a number of small and unique shops are located here. Visitors find vintage clothing, unusual fashion items, organic food, unique books, quirky gifts and rare antiques.
Notting Hill Website

Notting Hill Map

Markets in London

If you are looking for some interesting items to buy in West London, the Portobello Road Market is the perfect place for you. It is a very popular street market for locals and tourists alike. Hundreds of stalls filled with cheap trinkets, clothes, accessories, food, and souvenirs pile up along the two mile stretch of the Portobello road. It is usually busy during weekends, especially Saturday afternoons.

The Portobello Road Market started as a winding country path known as the Green Lane. In the 1850s, the marketplace started to take shape to accommodate families living in newly developed homes in Paddington and Notting Hill. From simple antiques to second-hand household items, the market expanded and expanded until it developed into what it is today.

The street market is divided into distinct sections. There is the antique's section that stretches from the Chepstow Villas to Eigin Crescent. From Eigin Crescent to Talbot Road, you will find stalls filled with fruits and vegetables. For cheap socks, laundry bags, and other everyday goods, visit the Westway.

Fashionable clothes and accessories can also be found on Westway, but other stalls are also scattered along the general side of the street. For second hand goods, the road from Westway to Golborne Road is lined up with stalls that sell these items.

Aside from shopping, there are also fun activities that one can do when visiting Portobello Road Market. There's the electric cinema where you can watch old and new movies while sitting comfortably in plush armchairs or two seat sofa. The Noting Hill Carnival, meanwhile, is a large street festival that is held every year during the August Bank Holiday.

Portobello Road Market Website

Portobello Road Market Map

Billingsgate Market

The United Kingdom is one of the best producers of the freshest and richest sea delicacies in the world. The Billingsgate market is a hub for fish enthusiasts to see all the most delicious underwater ingredients that the country has to offer.

As the country's largest inland fish market, it sells 25,000 tonnes of fish and other underwater products each year. In addition, 40% of the products sold were imported from abroad. The annual turnover rate of the market can reach up to £200 million.

Billingsgate Market covers a vast land that measures up to 13 acres and is totally self-contained. The main floor offers a large trading hall with 98 stands and 30 shops. These include cafes, a boiling room for shellfish, cold rooms, a freezer store, and an ice making plant. You can also meet catering suppliers and merchants that specialize in poultry, non-perishable products, and other services.

Almost every port in the United Kingdom delivers their goods to this market. Once the fishes reach the coast, they are transported by road and arrive on the market during the early hours of the morning. The imported goods are sent using through large refrigerated containers to maintain its freshness. Live imports such as lobsters or eels come from Canada and even as far away as New Zealand.

There is also several processed seafood that is on display. These include cured or smoked fish and roe, as well as prepared meals like fish soup, cooked shellfish, and pâtés.

If you wanted to learn the proper ways of cooking delectable seafood, you can also in the Billingsgate Seafood Training School. It offers several courses on fish recognition, knife skills, food presentation, cooking, as well as nutrition. It is located in the heart of the market.

The Billingsgate Market is open on Tuesday to Saturday. Trading begins at 5 a.m. to 8:30 p.m.

Billingsgate Market Website

Billingsgate Market Map

10

Music

West End Musicals

Experience the glitz and glamour of the theater by checking out the musical performances in the West End side of London.

The west end theaters are never quiet. Every night, the infrastructures are glowing with bright neon lights that signal and are filled with posters of the next main, theatrical attraction.

Most of the theater houses here are of late Victorian and Edwardian construction giving them a very classic yet elegant feel.

The West End stages are also home to the longest running musical performances such as Cats, Blood Brothers, The Phantom of the Opera, Jesus Christ Superstar, Lion King, and a whole lot more. If you wanted to see the best of London's culture and performing arts scene, the West end theaters are the most highly-recommended places to visit.

Email: customerservices@londontheatre.co.uk
Phone: +44 (0) 20 7492 0810
West End Musicals Website

Royal Opera House

The Royal Opera House is one of the finest opera houses and major performing arts venue in the United Kingdom. It is located in Covent Garden, central London. It is the home of the Royal Ballet, the Royal Opera, and the Royal Opera House Orchestra.

There are available guided tours, exhibitions, and fine displays of art to relish and look at.

The building itself has wide open space that will make you feel relaxed and comfortable. It is a perfect getaway from the hustle and bustle of the city.

There are many places that you can visit at the Royal opera House. The first is the Paul Hamlyn Hall. It is a mini crystal palace that was built using Victorian style engineering and ironwork. It used to be a flower market and a concert hall. But now, it is a hall that showcases costumes and other artifacts from previous plays.

The Crush Room, meanwhile, is home of the two popular divas in the 19th century – Australian soprano Dame Nellie Melba and the Italian coloratura soprano Adelina Patti. Their beautiful bust sculpture is located in this room.

If you feel a little bit famished, the Amphitheater Bar is just around the corner. Paintings from popular modern and contemporary artists line its walls, which will surely provide excitement to every art lover out there.

In addition, the amphitheater bar has a majestic terrace where you can view the London skyline. Here, you can see the London's Eye, Nelson's Column, Westminster's Cathedral, Waterloo Station, and numerous infrastructures from a distance.

The Royal Opera House is open daily from people who want to learn more about art and culture. From Mondays to Saturdays between 10 am and 3 pm, bars and restaurants in the venue are also open to accommodate customers.

Address:Bow St, London WC2E 9DD
Phone:+44 (0)20 7304 4000
Royal Opera House Website

Royal Opera House Map

11

Top 5 London Restaurants

TOP 5 LONDON RESTAURANTS

London is a great place for food lovers and those looking for food adventure. Street foods abound, with amazing flavors and great textures. There are the ever-present fish-and-chips on every corner and in every street. Aside from these, there are numerous budget-friendly restaurants that offer amazing food.

Dinner (Heston Blumenthal)

This is a light-filled restaurant located at the Mandarin Oriental. It is best known for its reinterpretation of British historic dishes, such as the Salmagundi of the 18th century (chicken, marrow bone and salsify) and the Taffety Tart (rose, apple, blackcurrant and fennel sorbet). Aside from great food, service and stories, the view of Hyde Park is definitely a great add-on.

Address:Mandarin Oriental Hyde Park
66 Knightsbridge,
London SW1X 7LA

Phone: +44(0)20 7201 3833
Dinner Website

Dinner Map

Coq d'Argent

This restaurant, Brasserie and bar is located at the rooftop of the pink-and-terracotta James Stirling building. During the week, the restaurant serves classic French cuisine. On the weekends, the atmosphere is relaxed with jazz music and a brunch menu.

Address:The Poultry, 1 Poultry, London EC2R 8EJ
Phone: 020 7395 5000
Coq d'Argent Website

Coq d'Argent Map

Bonds

The Bonds also doubles as an in-house dining for Thread-needles. It also has a separate entrance, which caters to a majority of traders and bankers, especially on Thursdays and Fridays.

The menu is modern European fare with an Asian twist. The interior also incorporates a few Asian accents, like exotic flowers and sleek wood. Bonds is rated as one of the hotels that offer best value in London.

Address:5 Threadneedle St, London EC2R 8AY
Phone: 020 7657 8144
Bonds Website

Bonds Map

Sweetings

This establishment is a reminder of the time when London was a place swarming with chaps wearing pinstripe suits and carried furled umbrellas. Sweetings is a 120-year-old restaurant that specializes in fish and seafood.

Address:39 Queen Victoria St, London EC4N 4SF
Phone: 020 7248 3062
Sweetings Website

Sweetings Map

Kitchen W8

This is one of London's sleek neighborhood restaurant, which opened in 2009. The interior is all smooth chairs and very sophisticated, with an atmosphere of "café au lait-bitter chocolate" type with a banquet seating. It is an opulent place to dine, which earned it a Michelin star in 2011. It was described as a place where English food is served with a French soul. It balances out its sophistication with a relaxed dining experience, BYO-style on Sunday evenings and set menus at great values.

71

Address:11-13 Abingdon Rd, London W8 6AH
Phone:020 7937 0120
Kitchen W8 Website

Kitchen W8 Map

12

Parks

One of the greatest things of London is the amazing parks all over the city.If you are staying in London for a few days, make sure to visit a few parks.Here is a list of my favorite parks in London:

Hyde Park

Hyde Park is probably the most famous park in London.The park is a famous venue for Music festivals and social gatherings.The park is Massive and is a favorite with cyclists, walkers and skaters.One of the famous landmarks in the park is the Princess Dianna Memorial Fountain.The park has almost 4000 trees and is a great place to relax and read a book.

Phone:0300 061 2000
  Hype Park Website

  Hyde Park Map

Richmond Park

Richmond Park is another massive park in London.The park is about 1,000 hectares.The park is famous for almost 600 deer walking freely in the park.The park has great views from the hill over the city.

  Phone:0300 061 2200
  Richmond Park Website

  Richmond Park Map

Greenwich Park

Greenwich Park is the oldest Royal Park in London and offers some of the best views in London.The Royal Observatory is located in the park.This park is also great for relaxing and taking a break from the busy city life.

Phone:0300 061 2380
 Greenwich Park Website

 Greenwich Park Map

St James's Park

St James's Park is close to 3 royal palaces.This big park is famous for its lake and the pelicans that live in it.The Horse Guards Parade is also located in this park.The Household

Cavalry, the British Army Regiment, is one of the Queens official Guard Regiments, and they can be observed in this park.

Phone:0300 061 2350
St James's Park Website

St James's Park Map

Clapham Common

Clapham Common is located in the south of London and is a great open space in the city.It's perfect for sports matches and is great social park for fun and games.The park has three ponds, tennis courts and grass pitches.If you want to have a great relaxing day with family and friends then visit Clapham Common.

Clapham Common Website

Clapham Common Map

13

Only in London

London is known for its one-of-a-kind take on everything- street fashion that veers off from the usual, high-end fashion that's truly unique and awe-inspiring, to the best beers and wonderful food. Aside from getting to experience modern urban living that bustles in a place with a rich ancient root, there are a few other things that visitors can experience only in London.

London is increasingly becoming popular for its pop-up events- whether a pop-up club, festival or restaurant. Pop-up is something that is set up in a few hours, makes a huge wave in the scene and then packs up when the sun goes up. Nobody ever really knows when they will see the club or restaurant again, or if they will get to see them again. This uncertainty makes the event even more exciting.

Popular
Kopparberg Urban Forest
This is a Critics' choice for pop-up club. This is a musical forest with a Scandinavian theme. It first landed in the

summer of 2014, in Dalston. It has recently announced a comeback for 2015, over in Hackney Wick. The program is packed with DJ sets and numerous gigs. Event goers are treated to an array of street food and 2 bars.

E-mail: info@kopparbergurbanforest.com

Website

Night Tales

This is another Critics' Choice. Night Tales helped the London population to make it through arduous winters. It is an incredible pop-up party filled with street food and creative cocktails with DJs spinning party music in the background.

Address:1-2 Hepscott Road

London E9 5EN

Website

Summer Tales

A spin-off of Night Tales held in summer. The party has a jungle theme, which runs for 15 weekends. True to the theme, there are numerous plush hammocks spread all over the party area, with rope swings and a terrace 20 meters wide where people can soak up the summer sun.

Website

Rhythm Parlour

This is another Critics' Choice. This one-of-a-kind pop-up monthly event offers beard-trimming and haircut with disco bliss in the background. The Rhythm Parlour is happening in

Rye Wax Records, inside Peckham's Bussey Building. Goers get treated to some trimming (hair, mustache or beard) by Ryan MacGregor and his team, with some cocktails, and music (house and funk). Definitely a true London-only experience.

Website

14

London's Best Bars and Pubs

London is one of the best places in the worlds to eat, drink, and be merry.Migrations, invasions and trade that span centuries have definitely influenced the food and bar scene in this old, yet modern city. There are just so many places to eat and drink that one can go to a different pub each day for a year and still not be able to go through all of them.

Difference Between a Pub and a bar?

Pubs are a very important part of British society.Going to a traditional Pub is one of those experiences that you have to have in London. British people love to be social, and there is no better place to grab beer after work with friends than a pub.

I often get asked what is the difference between a pub and a bar.The main difference between the two is that in a pub the atmosphere is more casual, and the food choices are usually better. It is common to have lunch or dinner in a pub, but not a bar. Bars will typically serve a wide variety of mixed drinks and liquors.For example, you might get cocktails at a bar, but not a pub.Pubs focus on a wide variety of beers and classic pub food.At a pub, you have to order food and drinks at the bar.Pubs do not offer table service.

Closing Hours:According to British law pubs close at 11 PM.You will hear the bell for last rounds at around 10:55 pm.

Bars have a different atmosphere than pubs. The music is louder, and the crowd is different.

Closing Hours:Most bars are open until 2 am because they have different rules, according to law.

Pubs

A visit to London won't be complete without a visit to some of the best traditional pubs in London.The pubs of the UK are unique and really gives you a sense of the great social dynamics in London.The pubs of London are where everybody from all walks of life gets together to have a pint of beer and talk about life.There are over 7000 pubs in London.I have picked out a few of the best traditional pubs in London.

Ye Old Mitre Tavern

This quaint old tavern is in Farrington, believed to be built in 1546 by Bishop Goodrich. This is a traditional tavern in every sense- cramped, 3-roof space, with stand-up tables in the enclosed courtyard out front. The tavern is accessible through alleyways branching from 2 separate streets.

The tavern offers ales with history:
- Caledonian 80
- George Gale Seafarers
- Adnams Broadside
- Deuchars IPA
- Fuller's Honeydew

There are also a few wines such as pinot grigio Veneto and pinot noir La Lumiere. Food is old-school pub such as:
- Pork pies
- Scotch eggs
- Toasted sandwiches
- And other full hearty meals

Address:1 Ely Pl, London EC1N 6SJ

Phone:020 7405 4751
Ye Old Mitre Tavern Website

Ye Old Mitre Tavern Map

The Viaduct Tavern

This pub is Located in the St Paul's area of London and is very central.It's located in a historic area and is opposite the Old Bailey.The pub is in a great area if you like to have a pint of beer in a historic area of London.The pub has a good variety of Ales on tap.This pub is a great place to drink a traditional English Gin and Tonic.The pub also has a good collection of wines.Th pub also serves traditional Engish pub food, from fish pie and beef stew to pie and mash.

Address:126 Newgate St, London EC1A 7AA
Phone:020 7600 1863
The Viaduct Tavern Website

The Viaduct Tavern Map

The George Inn

This pub is over 300 years old and is one of favorites to visit.This pub has an amazing atmosphere and is a great place for a party with friends or a leisurely Sunday pint of beer.The George has a fine variety of beer and food.The George Inn is South of the river and not very central but its well worth the trip.To get there by subway go to Southwark Station.

Address:The George Inn Yard, 77 Borough High St, Southwark, London SE1 1NH
Phone:020 7407 2056
The George Inn Website

The George Inn Map

The Lamb

This historic pub has a Victorian-style interior and is a great place to have a traditional pub experience in central London.The pub was build around 1729 and is has a great atmosphere.The pub serves a nice variety of traditional British pub food and has a good variety of Beer and Ale.The pub is located in central London in the Holborn area.To get there by subway go to Holborn Station.

Address:94 Lamb's Conduit Street
Bloomsbury London, WC1N 3Lz
Phone:0207 4050713
The Lamb Website

The Lamb Map

The Trafalgar Tavern

The Trafalgar Tavern in Greenwich is a riverside pub in Greenwich that is extremely popular with a great atmosphere.The Location of the pub next to the river makes it a great place to spend a summer day with friends and family.It has a nice beer and food menu and is definitely a must see when you go to Greenwich.To get there by train go to the Cutty Sark DLR train station.It is a 10 min walk from the station.

Address:Park Row, London SE10 9NW
Phone:020 8858 2909
The Trafalgar Tavern Website

The Trafalgar Tavern Map

Bars

The Beer Shop

Located in Nunhead, The Beer Shop is a popular watering hole among locals and tourists alike. It is a friendly bar that is also a shop. They have an extensive selection of different beers. The back counter of The Beer Shop dispenses 3 delicious draught beers. Notable are the pale ales, namely, citrusy Moor Top from Buxton Brewery and fruity and smooth Monacus by Northern Monk.

This watering hole also offers over 60 different ciders, porters and bottled beers. Most of these are from London brewers, whose beers all have succinctly clear tastes. Examples are the well-known Camden Town Hells and Brewdog. There are other beers like By The Horn's Sour to the People (sour-mash, burgundy-aged vintage beer) and the blended Ratchet artisan ale by Siren available in 750 mL bottles.

The Beer Shop is more like an extension of the locals' living rooms. Anyone can bring their takeaway food and the shop

85

happily supplies the beer. Everything in the shop is also available for takeaway. Fancy having draught beer takeaway in 2-pint containers.

Address:40 Nunhead Green, London SE15 3QF
Phone:020 7732 5555
The Beer Shop Website

The Beer Shop Map

15

Night Clubs

Let's take a look at the top clubs of London:

Ministry of Sound

The Ministry of Sound is one of the most popular British record labels and a big phenomenon in the dance music since ever since 1991.

For dancers and party goers, this venue located in Gaunt Street London provides the best sound system and music collection that will make your hips and entire body groove to the beat. Also, the club is illuminated by a dazzling light show that will make the music come alive.

The Ministry of Sound has five distinct rooms that you can explore. The 103 is the first room and is also known as the heart of the club. The Legendary Box, meanwhile, is the largest room in the club, this is also where the world's famous DJs gather and present their astonishing beats to partygoers.

The third room is the Baby Box. It is quite small compared to the other two venues, providing a more intimate party experience.

The Loft is the Ministry of Sound's newest lounge bar. This is an ideal place to catch up on the upcoming records labels and promoters before they even hit the music stores. Finally, there is the VIP lounge. It has private balconies where you can a splendid overlooking view of the headlining DJs. You only get access to this room through table bookings, DJs and their guest lists, providing a very exclusive and intimate feel.

Thanks to the latest refurbishments of the place, the Ministry of Sound now also boasts other amenities such as four bars, four dance floors, four DJ booths, and a new audiovisual specification.

Address:103 Gaunt St, London SE1 6DP
Phone:0870 060 0010
Ministry of Sound Website

Ministry of Sound Map

Studio 338

Studio 338 is one of the best and most popular clubs in London.Firstly this is the biggest club in London, so it has a lot of space.What makes the club special is that it has an outside terrace for clubbers to dance.If it's a cold night, you have the option of dancing on the heated terrace or move inside to the other dance floor.Studio 338 is famous for hosting World-class house and techno DJs.

Address:338 Boord St, London SE10 0PF
Phone:020 8293 6669

Studio 338 Website

Studio 338 Map

16

London in 3 Days

Itching to go to London? Try this 3-day sample itinerary to maximize the London experience:

Day 1:
Idea 1: Hop on the sightseeing bus to see all the iconic and historical landmarks such as the St. Paul's Cathedral. The ticket for the bus is valid for 24 hours. Visitors can hop on and off the bus throughout the validity of the ticket. Other sites to see for this tour are: grand London view from the Shard, the Tower of London, and the Tower Bridge. End the day with a show in London's West End.

Idea 2: Walk around the city and hop on a taxi to see: Trafalgar Square, witness the changing of the Guards at the Buckingham Palace, visit the Churchill War Rooms, go to the Big Ben and the Westminster Abbey. Take the London Eye and see the city change from its day view into its charming night scene.

Day 2:

Idea 1:Ride the London Eye and see the city by day, visit the Big Ben, the Houses of Parliament, the Westminster Abbey, National Gallery, the Buckingham Palace and the Piccadilly Circus

Idea 2: Visit theMuseum of London or the British Museum, St Paul's Cathedral, Covent Garden and, at the end of the day, see a show on West End.

Day 3

Idea 1: Visit 2 of the best museums in London such as the V&A, the Natural History Museum or the Science Museum. Do some shopping at Harrods and end the entire tour with a grand show at the Royal Albert Hall or The O2.

Idea 2: Visit the Tower Bridge, Tower of London, the Shard, HMS Belfast, Tate Modern. Then drop by Shakespeare's Globe Theater and end the tour with a treat at the Royal Festival Hall.

For Guided Tours In London CLICK HERE

17

PARIS INTRODUCTION

This book is for the traveler who has limited time and want to see the best Paris has to offer in 2 or 3 days.This book is about experiencing the best of the best in a short time

Paris is an amazing city, and one of the biggest mistakes people make when visiting a great city like Paris is to try and see everything in 2 or 3 days.The problem with this approach is that you end up running from one place to the next and not really experiencing the amazing energy of Paris.You end up being exhausted and wishing you could go home.

The best approach for short stay travelers is to focus on the best the city has to offer.This approach allows you experience the best and really soak up the unique energy of Paris.Take your time and relax.Don't turn travel into a stressful experience.

I hope this little book will help you to make your stay in Paris one of the best experiences of your life.Have a great time in the city of Love!

Good Luck!

18

Transportation and Safety

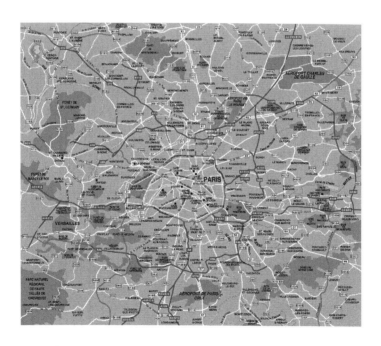

Getting Around Paris

The best way to get into Paris from Charles De Gaulle airport is to take the RER train that has several stops in central Paris and connects with the Metro System(Subway).

Paris International Airport Website

Paris International Airport Train Website

Paris International Airport Map

Since you only have a few days in Paris, I will recommend you use the Paris Metro(Subway) to get around the City.The Metro trains are a quick and easy way to get around the city and avoid traffic jams.The Paris Metro system has around 300 stations.The Metro (subway) runs every day from 6am to 0:30am.

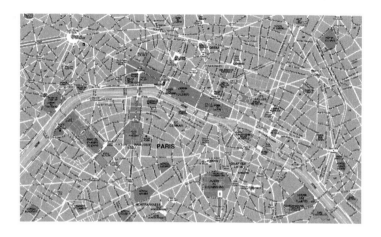

Paris Metro Website

If you find yourself in a situation in Paris where you can't find a taxi, or it's too late to take the subway then look for a Noctilien(Night bus).These busses run from 0:30am to 5:30 am.

Paris Night Bus Website

The cheapest way to get around the city is to buy a Paris transport travel card.This card will give you unlimited access to Metro, Bus and RER trains.

If you do decide to take taxis in Paris make sure the Taxi has the red illuminated "Taxi Parisien" sign on the roof and has a taxi meter inside the cab displaying the cost.Don't get into an illegal cab or your journey could end in a bad experience by being asked to pay a lot of money for a short journey.

Paris Transport Website

Safety

Paris is one of the safest cities in Europe when it comes to violent crimes.But crimes like pickpocketing is fairly common.If you are traveling alone be conscious of your surroundings, especially at night.

Let's look at some tips that you can follow to be safe in Paris:

(1)Never leave your bags and valuables unattended in public

areas like the bus or metro.

(2)Pickpocketing is fairly common in crowded places like the metro.So make sure your valuables like your wallet and passport is in a safe place.Don't carry too much cash on you and always leave a backup cash or credit card at your hotel.Pickpockets blend in well with the crowd and work in teams.They have been known to pretend to be a romantic couple shopping around.The Louvre Museum is also a very popular spot for pickpockets.So be on cautious!

(3)If you are traveling alone avoid the following areas at night:

-Les Halles, Chatelet, Gare du Nord and Stalingrad.
These areas have been known to have some gang activity.

-The Northern Paris suburbs of Saint-Denis, Aubervilliers, Saint-Ouen.
These areas have been known to have incidents of hate crimes recently so be careful.If you do walk around these areas avoid wearing jewelry or clothing representing any religion since these hate crimes are getting more common in some parts of Paris.

(4)Although Paris is a reasonably safe city, Women should especially be careful walking at night.Don't make too much-prolonged eye contact with men because it could, unfortunately, be seen as a sign of interest.So be aware of this.Remember also that Paris is a world city and that there are some foreign gang elements in France that speaks French fluently.So be cautious of strange men trying to take you to a place you don't know.

(5)Pedestrians should be careful in Paris.Drivers in France are very aggressive so be sure to look twice when crossing a busy road.

(6)If you find yourself in a dangerous situation and you need to call the Police dial "17"

19

Hotels

If you are visiting Paris for a couple of days, you better search for a place to stay. Here is a list of hotels that might strike your fancy.The first group of hotels are for the budget traveler,and the second for people who want to spend a bit more on accommodation.

Budget Hotels

· **Familia Hotel**

The Familia Hotel is a legendary Budget Hotel in Paris.If you are looking for something cosy and traditional, then this is the place for you.

Phone : +33 1 43 54 55 27
Address : 11 Rue des Écoles, 75005 Paris

Familia Hotel Website

· Hotel Arvor

Hotel Arvor is a stylish hotel , but in typical french style they manage to create a homely feeling that makes you feel like you are in a home away from home.

Phone :+33 1 48 78 60 92
Address : 8 Rue Laferrière, 75009 Paris

Website

· Port Royal Hotel

Port Royal Hotel is an amazing budget hotel in the Latin quarter of Paris.The reputation of this Hotel is legendary, and you will find an extremely clean room and great service.

Phone : +33 1 43 31 70 06
Address : 8 Boulevard de Port-Royal, 75005 Paris

Website

· Hotel Ecole Centrale

This hotel has a unique decoration style, and you will see plants and flowers everywhere.They have free wi-fi and all-round great service.The Hotel is very close to the trendy area Marais.

Phone : +33 1 48 04 77 76

Address : 3 Rue Bailly, 75003 Paris
Website

Hotel Ecole Centrale Website

Pricey Hotels
· **Hôtel Plaza Athénée Paris**

It is a hip and an extremely plush hotel that is located near the Eiffel Tower. It has a balcony that replete with red awnings. Inside the hotel, you will be greeted by warm bouquets of flowers.

One of the most sought-after areas in Hôtel Plaza Athénée Paris is the bar. It has an illuminated glass counter that resembles a very large iceberg.

If you need a little bit of rest and relaxation, you should visit the nearby Dior Institut Spa where you will be treated with a bevy of massages using the lush fragrances from the fashion company. Other amenities that you can find in the hotel include a music library that boasts of more than 5,000 tunes and a wine cellar that houses 35,000 different bottles.

Phone : +33 1 53 67 66 65
Address : 25 Avenue Montaigne, 75008 Paris

Website

· **Hotel Therese**

This is one of the very first and unique boutique hotels that you can find in the city of love. Hotel Therese is a favorite among fashion editors and enthusiasts because it is extremely close to the designer stores in the Palais-Royal. It is also near the Musée du Louvre.

The Hotel consists of 43 different rooms. The cheapest ones offer a sense of comfort and warmth even though they are slightly compact. Guests can also relax in the sitting rooms that were inspired by the works of Tom Dixon or Jean Jean Royère.

If you are searching for a room that is more expensive, you will definitely enjoy the classic and innovative architectural designs of Jean-Louis Deniot.

Phone : +33 1 42 96 10 01
Address : 5 Rue Thérèse, 75001 Paris

Website

· **Four Seasons Hotel George V**

The Four Seasons Hotel George V has been around since 1928. It has lasted throughout the ages because it showed elegance and luxury to its patrons.

Fashionable jet-setters flock towards this hotel because of

the several modern amenities that the hotel offers. In addition, the interior design is totally splendid. The marble lobby is lined with eye-catching blossoms. The ceilings are lined with crystal chandeliers, and the walls are covered in fine Flemish tapestries.

Phone : +33 1 49 52 70 00
Address : 31 Avenue George V, 75008 Paris

Website

· **Hotel Caron De Beaumarchais**

The design of the establishment still looks a little bit ancient and medieval. However, that does not mean that it lacks in modern amenities such as stylish bathrooms or internet hotspots.

This boutique hotel only has 19 rooms, and each of them has a classic French design. They are replete faux Louis XVI furnishings, and an intricate arrangement of trompe-l'oeil. The atmosphere of the hotel is very romantic.

Hotel Caron De Beaumarchais also has an indoor spa and a nearby pool that is surrounded by murals of Versailles. If you are feeling a little bit hungry, head over to Le Cinq. This two-star restaurant boasts of divine meals such as red tuna fillet, marinated vegetables and Manjari soufflé.

Address : 12 Rue Vieille du Temple, 75004 Paris

Phone : +33 1 42 72 34 12

Website

20

Historical Sites

Aside from being the City of Light, Paris is also a lovely city rich in culture and history. Paris is lavish in historical and monumental structures that are iconic and breathtaking. More than just the Eiffel Tower, this romantic city is popular for many other wondrous structures that evoke magnificent feelings in tourists and travelers in Paris. Check them out below:

· **Pantheon**

Located in the Latin Quarter, the Pantheon (which means "every god") is a neo-classical monument that is deemed to be the first of its kind. It was originally built as a replacement for the ruined Sainte-Genevieve Church under the order of Louis XV and assigned Jacques-Germain Soufflot as the chief architect. Soufflot combined gothic and classical principles in creating the structure, but all his plans were not carried out when he died just before the church was completed.

The Pantheon was first called as the new Sainte-Genevieve Church, but during the French Revolution, the Revolutionist government turned the massive church into a mausoleum for burying the outstanding Frenchmen that sacrificed their lives for the people. The Pantheon reverted back to being a church until it finally stayed as a place for burial for the martyrs and exceptional French citizens.

Phone : +33 1 44 32 18 00
Address : Place du Panthéon, 75005 Paris
Website

Pantheon Map

· **La Conciergerie**

The Concergerie has a rich history and has witnessed a thousand years of power play between great politicians and royalties. It was built within a Roman fortress and was part of the Palais de Justice before it was later turned into a court and prison during the French Revolution. La Conciergerie was used by the Revolutionary Tribunal to house their prisoners before their executions.This was the place where Marie Antoinette was kept before she was guillotined.

The Conciergerie is considered as one of the finest pieces of architecture during the Middle Ages. Some of the areas that you should totally visit are the guard room and Gens d'Armes. Drop by the northeastern region to see Paris' first ever public clock. It was installed in the area in 1370.

Phone : +33 1 53 40 60 80
Address : 2 Boulevard du Palais, 75001 Paris
Website

La Conciergerie Map

· **Père Lachaise Cemetery**

The Père Lachaise Cemetery was named after Père François de la Chaise, the confessor of Louis XIV. It was established by Napoleon in 1804, built on the site where the Jesuit priest lived, and designed by Alexandre-Théodore Brongniart. It is the most visited Parisian necropolis because of its tombs that are ornamented by monuments of every kind of funerary art style.

Even though it is a cemetery, it is still a fine place for a romantic date. That is because it is revered by many as one of the most poetic graveyards in the world. A lot of influential people are buried in its walls. Fans of The Doors usually pay their respect to Jim Morrison's grave. Literary figures such as Oscar Wilde, Richard Wright and even Molière are buried here.

Cemeteries are usually filled with a lot of grief and sadness. However, you will be surprised to discover that you can find joy in the cemetery's peak while viewing the lavish designs of the crypts.

Phone : +33 1 55 25 82 10
Address : 16 Rue du Repos, 75020 Paris
Website

Père Lachaise Cemetery Map

· Place de la Concorde

Known for this site's notoriety during the French Revolution, Place de la Concorde was the plaza for the execution of many prominent French. A total of 1119 people were beheaded using the guillotine that was installed in the center of the plaza.

Historical monuments abound the Place de la Concorde, including the statue of King Louis XV, the Liberte, the old obelisk from the temple of Ramses II at Thebes, the statues representing French cities (Bordeaux, Brest, Lille, Lyon, Marseille, Nantes, Rouen and Strasbourg), and the fountains "La fontaine des Mers" and "Elevation of the Maritime."

Address : 75008 Paris
Place de la Concorde Map

· La Sainte-Chapelle

Located near the Palais de la Cité, this beautiful medieval gothic chapel once housed the relic "Crown of Thorns" before it was relocated to the Notre Dame Cathedral. The chapel is a stunning house of vibrantly colored stained glass windows and majestic chandeliers. This historical site is revered by many as a top-notch Gothic wonder.

The entire area looks very delicate. As you try to traverse the chapel's vast aisles, it feels like you are actually inside a huge palace that is made from colored bits of glass. Its wall paintings and carvings are also a marvel to look at. It was constructed in order to store the crown of thorns that Jesus Christ had worn during his crucifixion. King Louis IX managed to buy this from Constantinople's emperor during the 13th century.

Phone : +33 1 53 40 60 80
Address : 8 Boulevard du Palais, 75001 Paris
Website

La Sainte-Chapelle Map

· **Opera Garnier(Palais Garnier)**

Originally called the Salle des Capucines because it was located on the Boulevard des Capucines, it was later named Palais Garnier after its architect, Charles Garnier. It is a large opera house for the Paris Opera and can seat 1,979 audiences then and now it can accommodate 2,200 people. This neo-baroque style architectural treasure is now home of the Paris ballet when the Paris Opera relocated to the Opera Bastille in 1989

Phone : +33 1 71 25 24 23
  Address : 8 Rue Scribe, 75009 Paris
  Website

Opera Garnier Map

· **Arc de Triomphe**

To commemorate the French soldiers, Napoleon commissioned the building of this monumental arch after their victory at the Battle of Austerlitz. This historical triumphal arch is richly engraved with inscriptions that chronicle the French military victories, including the names of the generals and the battles that were fought.

This 164-foot arch was built in order to stir up military dominance and victory against its enemies. You have to understand that Arc de Triomphe was constructed in a time when powerful leaders erect various monuments in order to honor their greatness, as well as to give themselves a massive ego boost.

Arc de Triomphe is a sight to behold because of the majestic sculptures that were carved on its arch. After you have seen the elegance of this massive site, you can head down to the luxurious avenue called the Champs-Elysees.

Phone : +33 1 55 37 73 77
Address : Place Charles de Gaulle, 75008 Paris
Website

Arc de Triomphe Map

· **Hôtel de Cluny and Roman Baths**

Hôtel de Cluny is located not far from the Sorbonne in the Latin Quarter. It was built on the ruins of the Gallo-Roman thermal baths, the Thermes de Cluny. The ruins remaining today constitute about one third of the original bath complex.

The hotel, which was once the town house of the abbots of Cluny, is a combination of Gothic and Renaissance art elements when it was rebuilt by Jacques d'Amboise. Today, the hotel houses the Musée du Moyen-Age or Musée de Cluny.

Phone : +33 1 53 73 78 00
Address : 6 Place Paul Painlevé, 75005 Paris
Website

Hôtel de Cluny and Roman Baths Map

· Crypte Archeologique Paris

Hidden underneath the Notre Dame Cathedral, the Crypte Archeologique of Paris can be accessed by a stairwell in the plaza. It houses the ruins of Lutetia, the Ancient Gallo-Roman town that existed before the place became known as Paris.

Phone : +33 1 55 42 50 10
Address : 7 Parvis Notre-Dame - Pl. Jean-Paul II, 75004 Paris
Website

Crypte Archeologique Paris Map

· The Sorbonne

The Sorbonne, founded and built in 1257, is one of Europe's oldest universities. It was built originally for theological studies because scholarship at that time was mostly a monastic domain.

It was first known as the Collège de Sorbonne before it was more famously known as the University of Paris. It was strictly a Catholic university until it was placed under Protestant control in the rule of King Francis I.

Phone : +33 1 40 46 22 11
Address : 75005 Paris
Website

The Sorbonne Map

· **Les Invalides**

Also known as L'Hôtel des Invalides, this structure is a complex of buildings that houses museums and is the site of Napoleon

Bonaparte's tomb. It was built in the seventeenth century to serve as a center of recuperation and refuge for injured soldiers under the order of King Louis XIV

Phone : +33 810 11 33 99
  Address : 129 Rue de Grenelle, 75007 Paris
  Website

Les Invalides Map

· The Latin Quarter

The Latin Quarter, or Quartier Latin, surrounds the Sorbonne. It is a massive plaza of scholastic activity that houses several institutions of higher education. The name of the place itself is reminiscent of the days of Bohemian Paris.

Address : Latin Quarter, 75005 Paris
The Latin Quarter Map

· **Notre Dame Cathedral of Paris**

If this is your first time to visit the city of love, then you should definitely pass by the Notre Dame Cathedral. Disney drew a stellar caricature of this place in their animated film called The Hunchback of Notre Dame. However, the actual cathedral is more marvelous in real life. The entire establishment is filled with dramatic flair because of its Gothic-inspired architecture.

Notre Dame Cathedral's sharp towers, stained glass windows and long spires will surely sweep you off your feet once you see them. A massive Gothic Cathedral built in 1163 in honor of the Virgin Mary. It now houses the "Crown of Thorns" relic, which was once kept in La Sainte-Chapelle. It is a towering structure along the Seine River that is ornate with breathtaking architectural details like the grotesques, gargoyles, and large stained-glass windows.

It had taken a century of extremely harsh labor before this infrastructure was completed. However, the worker's efforts were not in vain because the end result is a beauty to behold.

When you visit this cathedral, do not forget to climb the topmost part of the North Tower. The dazzling view of the city of love will make you realize why the Notre Dame Cathedral is considered as one of the best attractions in the area.

Phone : +33 1 42 34 56 10
Address : 6 Parvis Notre-Dame - Pl. Jean-Paul II, 75004 Paris
Website

Notre Dame Map

· **Palais Royal**

Formerly known as the Palais Cardinal, this beautiful palace was renamed Palais Royal when the cardinal bequeathed the whole place to King Louis XIII. It was almost destroyed by fire in 1871, leaving only the basic structure intact. It was reconstructed in 1876 and now houses the Council of State. The Palais Royal is located between the Opera Garnier and Musee du Louvre.

Phone : +33 1 47 03 92 16
Address : 8 Rue de Montpensier, 75001 Paris
Website

Palais Royal Map

· **The Catacombs of Paris**

The Catacombs were former mines before it was transformed into an underground graveyard in the eighteenth century.

These catacombs may not be one of the city's most romantic hot spots, but it is still a good place to visit if you want to have a little bit of a scare. During the 18th century, this labyrinth of bones was once a bustling underground mine. The catacomb of Paris houses a lot of sad tales from fallen soldiers and people who died during the French Revolution.

More than six million skeletons are kept in this area. If you are fit enough to climb at least 83 steps and if you do not have any claustrophobia, this is a travel destination that you should definitely not miss.

Phone : +33 1 43 22 47 63
　　Address : 1 Avenue du Colonel Henri Rol-Tanguy,
　　75014 Paris
　　Website

　　The Catacombs of Paris Map

· Hôtel de Ville

Once called "Place de la Grève," this Renaissance-style structure was a notorious place for executions. Its square has a gory
history of beheading, quartering, cooking up, and burning of
people at the stake until the installation of a guillotine. The
main hall building is decorated with statues that represent
famous Parisians and French cities. It now hosts different
events throughout the year.

Phone : +33 1 42 76 40 40
    Address : Place de l'Hôtel de Ville, 75004 Paris
    Hôtel de Ville Map
    · **Eiffel Tower**

The most iconic and popular landmark of Paris is the Eiffel Tower. Named after Gustave Eiffel, this structure was designed as part of a monument competition the Universal Exhibition World Fair and to celebrate the 100th anniversary of the French Revolution. It was originally built to last only 20 years, but it was continually reconstructed and improved to last throughout the last century.

This is considered as one of the most popular landmarks in Paris. That is because it has been featured in numerous television shows, print materials and films. This large iron tower was developed by Gustave Eiffel. It was meant to be presented to the World Exposition in 1889. Unfortunately, the Parisians from the early days did not appreciate the design of the tower. A lot of them even proposed to tear the tower down.

Thankfully, the people started to appreciate the beauty of the Eiffel Tower as time goes by. To this day, more than 200 million tourists have already visited this historical landmark. At night, you should definitely watch the majestic lights that glitter on top of the tower.

It would be very difficult to imagine what the city would look like without this very iconic infrastructure.

Phone : +33 892 70 12 39
Address :Champ de Mars, 5 Avenue Anatole France,
75007 Paris
Website

Eiffel Tower Map

· St. Denis Basilica

One of the oldest places for Christian worship in France, this Catholic basilica is located in St. Denis, a suburb in northern Paris. It is a Gothic structure that is popular for its stained-glass windows and for being a burial site for French monarchs.

Phone : +33 1 48 09 83 54
  Address : 1 Rue de la Légion d'Honneur, 93200 Saint-Denis
  Website

St. Denis Basilica Map

· **Memorial to the Martyrs of the Deportation**

This memorial place was constructed as a tribute to the 200,000 people who were killed in the Nazi death camps during World War II. It is located across the Notre Dame Cathedral along the banks of the Seine River. The Deportation Memorial was designed by GH Pingusson and evokes a sense of despair and claustrophobia.

<u>Phone :</u> +33 1 46 33 87 56
<u>Address :</u> Allée des Justes de France, 75004 Paris
Website

Memorial to the Martyrs of the Deportation Map

· **<u>Louvre</u>**

The Louvre is a historic monument and landmark of Paris. It displays a wealth of artifacts in the Louvre Museum. The building was originally built as a fortress by King Philip II in the 12th century.It was a palace for the household of monarchs until King Louis XIV relocated to the Palace of Versailles and left the Louvre as a primary place for displaying royal collections.

It takes more than a day in order to traverse the entire Louvre and see everything that it has to offer; but for starters, you should definitely go and visit Mona Lisa or the majestic Venus de Milo.

Phone : +33 1 40 20 50 50
Address : 75001 Paris
Website

Louvre Map

· **Place de la Bastille**

The Bastille prison once stood here, and it's storming on July 14, 1789, signaled the start of the French Revolution. In 1794, the revolutionary authorities beheaded 75 enemies of the state with its guillotine. Today the Bastille Square remains a powerfully symbolic site for Parisians and many marches and demonstrations start or finish here.

<u>Address :</u> Place de la Bastille, 75011 Paris

Place de la Bastille Map

21

Museums and Galleries

Although many people believe that New York or Berlin has beaten Paris in terms of artistic dominance, the city is still a beautiful place that is teeming with inspiration, colors, museums and passionate artists.What makes Paris different from New York and Berlin is that everyday life is full of artistic expression.

In addition, the city is also dedicated to preserving their artistic inheritance and exposing them to locals and tourists alike. Their galleries and museums house some of the world's most vital and richest masterpieces.

If you are interested in learning more about Paris' artistic legacy, check out some of the best galleries and museums that you should visit. Make sure that you purchase a Paris Museum Pass to make your museum hopping experience easier and fun.

Paris Pass Website

· **Louvre Museum**

As mentioned earlier, the Louvre houses a museum that displays a wealth of artifacts. It is also the world's largest, most visited museum. It houses a massive collection of artworks from different centuries of Parisian and French history, culture, and traditions.

It is also home to artifacts from different historical places around the world and masterpieces of artistic European geniuses.

It takes more than a day in order to traverse the entire Louvre and see everything that it has to offer; but for starters, you should definitely go and visit Mona Lisa or the majestic Venus de Milo.

The Musée du Louvre is considered as one of the most diverse and biggest collection of paintings, decorative items, sculptures and other pieces of artwork from the pre-20th century era. In here, you can witness various masterpieces from renowned artists such as Caravaggio, Vermeer, and a whole lot more.

The historical infrastructure even tells a tale of rich history that spanned from the wonderful medieval ages up to the current era. If you feel weary from viewing paintings and sculptures, you can head towards the nearby Tuileries garden to relax and inhale a breath of fresh air.

Phone : +33 1 40 20 50 50
Address : 75001 Paris
Website

Louvre Museum Map

· **National Museum of Modern Art (MNAM).**

Pompidou, the National Museum of Modern Art is one of the world's most prestigious centers of modern art collections. It is home to more than 50,000 artworks from popular painters, sculptors, and architects of the 20th century like Picasso, Braque, Pollock. One factor that makes the MNAM a place worth many revisits is their practice of annual re-hanging and re-circulating of artwork displays.

The building itself boasts of innovative and stunning hi-tech architecture courtesy of popular designers Richard Rogers and his friend, Renzo Piano. When the Pompidou was finished in 1977, a lot of the Parisians adored the unique design of the establishment.

However, the vast collection of artworks is more exciting than the actual building. Inside, you will be able to view the masterpieces from contemporary artists such as Picasso and Matisse. On the next aisle, there are surrealist paintings.

In addition, there are also other amenities inside the Centre Georges Pompidou such as children's gallery, performing arts center and a cinema. If you want to bring home some souvenirs, you can visit the nearby design shop and art bookstore.

Lastly, fill your hungry stomach in the Georges restaurant once you are finished sightseeing.

Phone : +33 1 53 67 40 00
Address : 11 Avenue du Président Wilson, 75116 Paris
Website

National Museum of Modern Art Map

· **Musée d'Orsay**

Originally a train station designed by Victor Laloux, the Musée d'Orsay now houses art collections of the 19th and 20th centuries like Monet and Van Gogh. It is located across the Louvre, along the banks of the Seine River.

Phone :+33 1 40 49 48 14

<u>Address</u> : 1 Rue de la Légion d'Honneur, 75007 Paris
Website

Musée d'Orsay Map

· **Grand Palais**

The Grand Palais was built for the 1900 Exposition Universelle. It houses galleries of different art collections that are open for temporary exhibits. It also hosts art fairs and galleries for science and natural history.

Website

Grand Palais Map

· **Petit Palais**

Located just across the road from the Grand Palais, the Petit Palais showcases art works of about 1.300 from early centuries to the modern 20th century. The admission to the permanent exhibits is free, but the temporary exhibits are free only to visitors under 13 years of age.

Phone : +33 1 53 43 40 00
    Address : Avenue Winston Churchill, 75008 Paris

Website

Petit Palais Map

· Musee d'Art Moderne de la Ville de Paris

Housed in the Palais de Tokyo, the city of Paris' museum of modern art features more than 8,000 contemporary art works of the 20th and 21st centuries. It constantly hosts temporary exhibits, including photography works of modern photography artists.

Phone : +33 1 53 67 40 00
Address : 11 Avenue du Président Wilson, 75116 Paris
Website

Musee d'Art Moderne de la Ville de Paris Map

· Cité de l'Architecture et du Patrimoine

Built as an architecture and heritage museum, it features galleries of life-size mock-ups of facades of different cathedrals and heritage buildings. It also houses a gallery of full-scale copies of stained-glass windows and murals of medieval and Renaissance structures. Another highlight of their exhibits is the walk-in apartment replica of Le Corbusier's Cité Radieuse in Marseille.

Phone : +33 1 58 51 52 00
Address : 1 Place du Trocadéro et du 11 Novembre, 75116

Paris
Website

Cité de l'Architecture et du Patrimoine Map

· **Musée du Quai Branly**

Located at the banks of the Seine River, this museum houses ethnic arts of non-European cultures. It features a treasure of contemporary indigenous art and 10th century anthropomorphic statues.

Phone : +33 1 56 61 70 00
Address : 37 Quai Branly, 75007 Paris
Website

Musée du Quai Branly Map

· **Musée du Moyen-Age**

Also known as Musée de Cluny, this museum is housed within the Hôtel de Cluny. This gallery is dedicated to the art works of the medieval period. Its grounds also feature a garden that mimics the aromatic and medicinal gardens of the medieval times.

True to its name, the National Medieval Museum is a gallery that houses a vast collection of relics from the medieval times. It aims to explore the types of art that sprang during this era and retells the stories of how the people live during the great

"Moyen Age."

The most prized possession in the museum is a tapestry called The Lady and The Unicorn. It was created in the 15th century and it gained immense popularity because of its symbolism and a striking array of colors.

Phone :+33 1 53 73 78 00
Address : 6 Place Paul Painlevé, 75005 Paris
Website

Musée du Moyen-Age Map

· **Rodin Museum**

This museum features an extensive garden of sculptures by the French sculptor Auguste Rodin.

As you view some of his works such as the Balzac, Burghers of Calais, and the Gates of Hell, you will discover how this man revolutionized the art of sculpting during the 1900s. It is also exciting to learn how he frequently reused some of his previous sculptures in his next works.

The Musée National Rodin also houses some of the master-pieces from his student, Camille Claudel. The chapel is usually busy with temporary exhibitions. If you are looking for a place to relax, there is a lovely café located near the garden.

Phone : +33 1 44 18 61 10
Address : 79 Rue de Varenne, 75007 Paris
Website

Rodin Museum Map

· **Musée Carnavalet**

Also known as the Museum of Paris History, the Carnavalet Museum houses collections of historical artifacts and items that trace Paris' complex history in over 100 chronological rooms. Admission to the exhibits is free for all visitors.

Phone : +33 1 44 59 58 58
Address : 16 Rue des Francs Bourgeois, 75003 Paris
Website

Musée Carnavalet Map

· **Musée du Luxembourg**

Located in the luxuriant Luxembourg Gardens, the Luxembourg museum is one of Europe's oldest museums. It hosts temporary exhibits annually and focuses on paintings by French artists.

Phone : +33 1 40 13 62 00
Address : 19 Rue de Vaugirard, 75006 Paris
Website

Musée du Luxembourg Map

· **Musee Jacquemart-André**

The Jacquemart-André museum was founded by art collector, Edouard André and his artist wife Nélie Jacquemart. Its galleries focus on the works of French painters of the 18th and 19th century.

Phone : +33 1 45 62 11 59
Address : 158 Boulevard Haussmann, 75008 Paris
Website

Musee Jacquemart-André Map

· **Musée des Arts Décoratifs**

This decorative arts museum features one of the world's massive collections of design art. The primary focus of the museum is the French furniture and tableware. There are other galleries that are categorized by glass, drawings, toys, and wallpaper themes.

Phone : +33 1 44 55 57 50
Address : 107 Rue de Rivoli, 75001 Paris
Website

Musée des Arts Décoratifs Map

For Guided Tours in Paris CLICK HERE

22

Restaurants

The city of Paris is a haven for people who enjoy eating a

wide variety of dishes. Aside from the famous culinary dishes from France, most restaurants in the city also serve specialty meals from other countries. The chefs here can replicate your favorite dishes to make you feel closer to home, but they also add a little bit of a twist to each of them to make you appreciate the culture in Paris.

A lot of people think that the city is all about fine dining. Well, it is true that numerous five-star restaurants reside in this place. However, that does not mean that you cannot find some bistros that offer delicious meals at a lower cost. Here is a list of the best eateries, cafés and restaurants that you should definitely visit in Paris:

· **Boco**

Boco is a small chain of eateries that is located along the heart of the city. The famous three-star chefs such as Regis Marcon and Anne-Sophie Pic were the ones who developed the recipes that were placed in the restaurant's menu.

Most of their main dishes, appetizers and desserts were all made from organic ingredients so you have an assurance that what you will eat is fresh, delicious and healthy. Furthermore, their packaging is also eco-friendly. True to its name, this restaurant serves most of its dishes in reusable glass jars.

When you visit this place, you should definitely try Chef Pic's coddled eggs, Chef Renaut's mushroom and polenta lasagna, or Chef Philippe's mouth-watering pistachio crumble topped with a thick cream made from black sesame.

Phone : +33 1 42 61 17 67

Address : 3 Rue Danielle Casanova, 75001 Paris
Website

Boco Map

· **Relais d'Entrecôte**

If you are looking for a charming and hassle-free restaurant, this joint is ideal for you. Relais d'Entrecôte is famous for its rich steak frites dish. It is served with a secret sauce that will make your mouths water.

Do not be fooled if your first serving seems a little bit scant. The wait staff in the area is willing to provide you with second helpings of your dish if you want more.Aside from their famous steak frites, you will also enjoy the restaurant's light ambience, brasserie-inspired interior decorations and very accommodating waiters.

Phone : +33 1 46 33 82 82
Address :101 Boulevard du Montparnasse, 75006 Paris
Website

Relais d'Entrecôte Map

· **Verjus**

This exclusive restaurant is built by an American couple who were famous for their dinner club called the Hidden Kitchen. This place offers a private haven for romantic couples to enjoy each other's company while they are in the city of love.

The menu of Verjus consists of top-notch dishes that are made from seasonal and well-picked produce. If you are searching for a nice place where you can eat fried chicken, this is the restaurant that you should visit; and if you need to enjoy a bottle of fine spirits, feel free to peruse some of their liquor collections in their very own wine bar.

Phone : +33 1 42 97 54 40
Address : 52 Rue de Richelieu, 75001 Paris
Website

Verjus Map

· **Huitrerie Regis**

Huitrerie Regis is located in the middle along Saint Germain des Pres. This is the finest establishment to visit in Paris if you are craving for fresh oysters. That is because their seafood ingredients directly came from the country's Marennes-Oléron area which is located on the coasts of the Atlantic.

Depending on the season, they also serve prawns and sea urchins with bread on the side. You can complement your undersea dishes with a nice bottle of white wine from the Loire valley. The atmosphere of the place is also warm, so you can greatly enjoy your bivalve-centric meals.

Phone : +33 1 44 41 10 07
Address : 3 Rue de Montfaucon, 75006 Paris
Website

Huitrerie Regis Map

· **Macéo**

Maceo is operated by Mark Williamson – an English gentleman who also runs the popular local establishment called Willi's Wine Bar. Upon entering the restaurant, you will be greeted with its fine interior decorations that are composed of oxblood walls and floors that are made of parquet. You will also have a stunning view of the city's famous site called Palais Royal.

Chef Thierry Bourbonnais, the one who plans the menu of Macéo, offers several vegetable meals for the hungry vegetarian tourists. You will surely enjoy his scallop dish that is marinated using seaweed oil. The restaurant also serves a healthy plate of sea bass that is replete with mage toute, spicy bulghur and baby carrots. Lastly, they have a vast collection of vintage wines and spirits.

Phone : +33 1 42 97 53 85
Address : 15 Rue des Petits Champs, 75001 Paris
Website

Macéo Map

· **La Cantine de la Cigale**

Located in Pigalle, this place offers a fine array of specialty dishes from the south-west region of France. The restaurant is owned by bistro expert Christian Etchebest.

This cozy place is ideal for those worn-out travelers who are looking for a place to rest after an intense shopping spree. La Cantine de la Cigale's menu is replete with affordable but large portions of paâté, sausage and white bean platter, cherry jams, Mirabelle tarts, and a whole lot more.

Phone : +33 1 55 79 10 10
Address : 124 Boulevard de Rochechouart, 75018 Paris
Website

La Cantine de la Cigale Map

· **Le Coq Rico**

A French cuisine restaurant located at the top of Montmartre butte that specializes in delicious French chicken recipes. From breakfast to dinner, you will enjoy the assortment of homely meals that are worth savoring.

Phone : +33 1 42 59 82 89
Address : 98 Rue Lepic, 75018 Paris
Website

Le Coq Rico Map

· **Bistro Volnay**

Located near the Opera Garnier, Bistro Volnay is popular with businessmen, Parisians, and tourists alike. Their art deco-inspired place makes it a very warm and inspiring spot to eat, relax, and enjoy.

Phone : +33 1 42 61 06 65
Address : 8 Rue Volney, 75002 Paris
Website

Bistro Volnae Map

· **Chez L'Ami Jean**

This is a well-known Basque venue restaurant for their tasty and diverse French recipes that are very popular. From meat to seafood, you will find any dish in their menu very much worth a try.

Phone : +33 1 47 05 86 89
Address : 27 Rue Malar, 75007 Paris
Website

Chez L'Ami Jean Map

· **La Pulpéria**

The perfect place for meat lovers, this restaurant is known for their diverse menus that change every day. The meat recipes are cooked flavorfully and look sinfully indulging.

Phone : +33 1 40 09 03 70
Address : 11 Rue Richard Lenoir, 75011 Paris
Website

La Pulpéria Map

- **Breizh Café**

This crêperie is not a regular dessert station. Their choices of crepe fillings may be limited, but they use ingredient of the highest quality, and they offer a savory sea-side experience with their seafood recipes.

Phone : +33 1 42 72 13 77
Address : 109 Rue Vieille du Temple, 75003 Paris
Website

Breizh Café Map

- **Le Flamboire**

If you love barbecues, then this is the place to eat. This is where meat lovers flock to eat and enjoy flavorful and savory grilled meat dishes.

Phone : +33 6 95 01 77 38
Address : 54 Rue Blanche, 75009 Paris
Website

Le Flamboire Map

- **Frenchie To Go**

A takeaway sandwich bar that you will truly love. The queues are long though, so you have to be patient to get a bite of their well-known snacks.

Phone : +33 1 40 26 23 43
Address : 9 Rue du Nil, 75002 Paris
Website

Frenchie To Go Map

· Urfa Dürüm

A Kurdish sandwich shop that is said to be the best place for eating street food in Paris. This small but welcoming place will make you anticipate for their delicious Lahmacun and Dürüm.

Phone : +33 1 48 24 12 84
Address : 58 Rue du Faubourg Saint-Denis,
75010 Paris
Website

Urfa Dürüm Map

· Miznon

Street food never looked so good in Paris. Miznon is a restaurant that serves casual western-style French foods that are worth trying, particularly their pita sandwiches.

Phone : +33 1 42 74 83 58
Address : 22 Rue des Ecouffes, 75004 Paris
Website

Miznon Map

23

Shopping Districts

Your trip to the city of love will never be complete without a little bit of shopping. As you work your way around the busy streets of the city, you will discover that a lot of the locals find it so easy to look so fabulous and fashionable. It is no wonder that this city is still a center for everything couture. Next to historical landmarks, the shopping districts in Paris draw millions of tourists every year.

Whether you are a fashion victim, bargain hunter, window shopper or high-fashion diva, there is always a shop that will surely satiate your desires. Check them out below.

- **Sophie Sacs**

This boutique is popular for its low prices and huge sales, especially on bags. This establishment has been up and running ever since it opened in 1976, and has remained popular and crowded by people from all over Paris.

Phone : +33 1 45 48 00 69
Address : 149 Rue de Rennes, 75006 Paris
Website

Sophie Sacs Map

- **La Boutique de Louise**

Specializing in girly accessories, this boutique is popular for its affordable but cute accessory items like printed cushions, necklaces and pendants, bracelets, and fun items for your home.

Phone : +33 1 45 49 07 92
Address :32 Rue du Dragon, 75006 Paris
Website

La Boutique de Louise Map

· **Beau Travail**

A designer boutique formed by four aspiring and talented local designers who opened their couture creations to the public in the heights of Belleville. Displaying their creations with amazing price tags, Beau Travail, however, is only open to the public on schedule or by appointment.

Phone : +33 1 43 67 33 86
Address : 131 Rue de Bagnolet, 75020 Paris
Website

Beau Travail Map

· **Haili**

Established by former stylist Patricia Wang, this boutique features designer clothes of diverse varieties. She also carries new designer names from other parts of Europe every season. Additionally, Patricia herself can happily offer styling advice to her customers.

Phone : +33 1 40 47 54 86
Address : 56 Rue Daguerre, 75014 Paris, France
Haili Map

· **Paperdolls**

This boutique by Candy Miller offers everything girly from

chic apparels, handbags, and shoes. Her boutique features works from independent designers only. The highlight of this shop is the apartment–lie interior that divides the place into apartment rooms like a dining room, bathroom, and living room.

Phone : +33 1 42 51 29 87
Address : 5 Rue Houdon, 75018 Paris
Website

Paperdolls Map

· Anne Willi

This boutique by Anne Willi is great for finding and shopping for items that match different curves and personalities. The designs and materials are contemporary and will fit any occasion.

Phone : +33 1 48 06 74 06
Address : 13 Rue Keller, 75011 Paris
Website

Anne Willi Map

· Annabel Winship

Popular shoe boutique that features designs that think out of the box. If you quirky and fantastical shoe designs are your thing, this shop will be worth a visit.

159

Phone : +33 1 71 37 60 46
Address : 29 Rue Dragon, 75006 Paris
Website

Annabel Winship Map

Shopping Areas

Let's take a look at some of the best areas in Paris to go shopping.If you just want to take a walk and do some window shopping then I have a few suggestions for you:

· **Louvre-Tuileries and the district of Faubourg Saint-Honoré**

These places are ideal for tourists who are looking for top-notch cosmetics, designer clothes, and even stylish home furnishings. The district of Faubourg Saint-Honoré is always teeming with people because this is where most of the city's top fashion stores are placed. These include Yves Saint Laurent, Versace and even Hermes.

However, you can also search for popular concept shops here.
On the other hand, the Boulevard Haussmann is located in the neighborhood of Louvre-Tuileries. This is considered as the department store region of Paris.

Address : 113 Rue de Rivoli, 75001 Paris
Louvre-Tuileries and the district of Faubourg Saint-Honoré Map

· The Avenue of Montaigne and des Champs-Elysées

These two avenues form one of Paris' most sizzling fashion junctures. Legendary brands such as Chanel or Dior line the streets of Avenue Montaigne. Meanwhile Champs- Elysées showcases luxury brands and global chains such as Zara and Louis Vuitton. Both of these avenues are ideal if you are searching for the trendiest chain stores and designer items.

The Avenue of Montaigne and des Champs-Elysées Map
https://goo.gl/maps/C16RJ5MrE4K2

· Paris Flea Markets

The most popular and largest flea market in the city of love is called Saint-Ouen flea market. This area has been around since the 1900s. It is located in the northernmost part of Paris.

You can visit this place if you want to search for antique home furnishings, oddball objects, vintage apparel and discounted shoes.

Since this is a flea market, one should expect that every inch of the street will be filled with a lot of people during the weekends. So if you want to shop in peace and experience the beauty of the surroundings, it is best if you visit the place during weekends.

Paris Flea Markets Map

· **Avenue des Ternes**

Avenue des Ternes is a shopping hub that is not yet extremely popular with the tourists. This means that you can easily get first dibs on the rarest and most fashionable pieces of apparel that are available.

Even though the avenue does not attract a lot of tourists, it does not mean that the place is barren.

It is also a busy and colorful avenue because locals tend to shop here. Aside from clothing, you will find stores that sell home appliances, books, films, music and food. When you get tired from walking and buying, you can take a break in the nearby brasseries, coffee shops and bakeries.

Avenue des Ternes Map

· **Montmartre**

Similar to the flea market, Montmartre is also replete with stores that sell affordable pieces of jewelry, shoes, and clothing. The best places to visit are rue des Abbesses, rue Houdon, as well as rue des Martyrs.

If you want to find the cheapest deals, you can head towards Montmartre's eastern region where the working class neighborhood of Barbès is located. In here, you will find a large department store called Tati. This place offers quality apparel with huge discounts.

Montmartre Map

· **The Marais**

Once a historical area, the quarters of the Marais have become a center for shoppers with a passion for unique and eclectic fashionable items. In addition, you will also find a load of antique objects and fine pieces of artwork in this place. For art enthusiasts, one of the most highly recommended areas to visit is Place de Vosges.

For people who have an eye for fine jewelry, they can shop at boutiques such as Satellite located near Rue des Francs-Bourgeois. And if you are looking for the next fashion trends, head down towards Rue des Rosiers.

The Marais Map

· **Opéra & Grand Boulevards**

Located in the heart of Opéra & Grand Boulevards are two of the most sought-after department stores in the city– Galeries Lafayetteand the Printemps. Over the years, these large behemoths have built a vast neighborhood of discount shops around them. The most ideal stores in the area are located in the northernmost boulevards such as rue de Provence and rue Caumartin. They sell shoes, jewelry and clothes at extremely affordable prices.

Opéra & Grand Boulevards Map

24

Paris Bars

· **Silencio**

Silencio is hard to put in words, but in typical French style it's something truly unique.It could be described as a cross between an art nightclub and members only bar.The club is located underground and has a stage and a smoking room.Before midnight, only members of the club is allowed,but after midnight its free to go in for a limited number of people.A night at Silencio is something you will always remember.

Phone : +33 1 40 13 12 33
Address : 142 Rue Montmartre, 75002 Paris
Silencio Website

Silencio Map

· Candelaria

You will find Candelaria in a narrow street in Marais area of Paris.In the front of Candelaria, you can buy Mexican snacks like Tacos.However, if you go through the back door of Candelaria, you will find a fantastic cocktail bar.

Phone : +33 7 53 79 68 25
Address : 52 Rue de Saintonge, 75003 Paris
Candelaria Website

Candelaria Map

· Charlie

If you want to combine cocktails and art, then go the Charlie.The bar is a trendy up-and-coming hang out in Paris.Charlie has art exhibitions and live music that create a unique atmosphere.Charlie is another one of those places where you walk away thinking you will only experience a place like that in Paris.

Phone : +33 1 53 33 02 67
Address : 29 Rue de Cotte,Paris
Charlie Website

Charlie Map

25

Coffee

People think about many things when they come to Paris, but one thing they always dream about is having an amazing cup of coffee in one of Paris's best coffee shops.I have made a list of some of the best and unique coffee experiences in Paris:

- **Café des 2 Moulins**

This coffee shop gained immense popularity among tourists when it appeared in Jean-Pierre Jeunet's cult movie called Amélie. Even though it has been more than a decade since the film's release, this is still a popular tourist destination. That is because the café's ambience is very warm and cozy.

You will surely enjoy its vintage atmosphere, comfortable sitting room and relaxing cup of coffee. And once you are finished with this place, feel free to immerse yourself in the colorful market outside the café.

Phone : +33 1 42 54 90 50
Address : 15 Rue Lepic, 75018 Paris

Website

Café des 2 Moulins Map

· La Caféothèque

The name of this establishment means "coffee library" in English. True to its name, La Caféothèque is a highly recommended place for coffee enthusiasts who want to veer away from the cups of espresso at Starbucks. This shop imports their coffee beans from various plantations outside the country.

There is a large coffee roaster at the shop's front, and the scents of the beans always fill the place with delicious aroma. These raw ingredients are brewed well by adept baristas. In addition, they only use the finest espresso machines from the popular maker named La Marzocco.

La Caféothèque is located across Ile Saint-Louis. It is owned by Guatemalan coffee expert named Gloria Montenegro.

Phone : +33 1 53 01 83 84
Address : 52 Rue de l'Hôtel de ville, 75004 Paris
Website

La Caféothèque Map

· Café de Flore

This little coffee shop was once a cozy hub where intellects and artists gather and share ideas with their peers. The author, Charles Maurras, got the inspiration for his novel Au Signe de Flore in this place. Poets such as Guillaume Apollinaire and Louis Aragon sought refuge at Café de Flore when they felt the need to scribble some lines and verses. Even American authors such as Trauman Capote and Arthur Koestler even visited this humble coffee shop.

These days, Café de Flore is still a place where you can sip your favorite blend of coffee, meet fellow intellectuals and discuss some ideas with them.

Phone : +33 1 45 48 55 26
Address : 172 Boulevard Saint-Germain, 75006 Paris
Website

Café de Flore Map

· **Telescope Coffee**

This shop serves amazing coffee.The coffee shop has a minimalist style, and you won't find many better places drink excellent coffee in a very relaxing environment.The people who run this store take their coffee very seriously, and if you are a bit of a coffee addict like me then you will love this place.

Address : 5 Rue Villedo, 75001 Paris
Website

Telescope Coffee Map

· **The Broken Arm**

The Broken Arm is a Scandinavian style coffee shop in the trendy Marais area.The owners combine their three passions of coffee,design and fashion.The coffee served in the Broken arm is excellent and has an edgy atmosphere.

Phone : +33 1 44 61 53 60
Address : 12 Rue Perrée, 75003 Paris
Website

The Broken Arm Map

· **Cafe Le Look**

If you like a vintage cafe with a lot of character, then go and drink a cup of coffee at Le Look.This place has an amazing breakfast and also serve beer.

Phone : +33 9 50 10 20 31
Address : 17 Rue Martel, 75010 Paris
Website

Cafe Le Look Map

26

Sample 3 Day Itinerary

Try this 3-day sample itinerary to get the most out of your Paris experience:

Day 1:
Hop on the sightseeing bus to see all the iconic landmarks

such as the Pantheon. Visitors can hop on and off while the ticket is valid.You have unlimited use of the ticket over 1 or 2 days. Other sites to see for this tour are the Louvre, the Eiffel Tower and many others.

Walk around the city and hop on a taxi to see the the Bastille, the Picasso Museum and have a cup of coffee at the The Broken Arm. Have dinner and cocktails at Candelaria.
- **Day 2:**

Go to the trendy Marais area.Walk around and see the Bastille, the Picasso Museum and have a cup of coffee at the The Broken Arm. Have dinner and cocktails at Candelaria.
- **Day 3**

SAMPLE 3 DAY ITINERARY

Go to the Avenue of Montaigne and des Champs-Elysées. Have a fantastic day of shopping and enjoy the fashion experience of a lifetime.After shopping go to Montmartre and see the Basilica of the Sacred Heart of Paris(Sacre Coeur).Have a cup of coffee at the famous Cafe des 2 Moulins in Montmartre.

27

AMSTERDAM INTRODUCTION

Thank you for downloading my book. This book focuses on the Short Stay Traveler. If your time is limited in this wonderful city, then this book is perfect for you. I have put together the best Amsterdam has to offer in 3 to 4 days.

Amsterdam has a long, rich history behind it. It rose from simple beginnings and has become one of the best-planned cities of the modern world. It became the economic center of an entire nation at one time in the 17th century. And yet it owes its existence from a few simple fishing folk who just wanted to live a carefree life that has very little trouble.

Amsterdam is one of those special cities in the world that everyone knows about.It's usually one of the first recommendations of places to visit when someone travel to Europe.The reason is simple, Amsterdam is one of the most interesting places on this beautiful planet.

Amsterdam is an amazing mix of beautiful, old, new, interesting,unique,edgy,mysterious,cutting edge, modern and at times, strange.This fantastic mix of qualities creates one of the leading cities in Europe with a very interesting history.

Have a great time in Amsterdam!!

28

Amsterdam's Early Beginnings

The beginnings of Amsterdam

The beginnings of Amsterdam can be traced all the way to the 12th century. From the years 1150 to 1300, the locals who settled in the area took every effort to build dams. The idea was to contain the waters of the IJ River. The area to be covered ranged from Haarlem all the way to Zuiderzee. During this time, a small community of fishing folk began to form on the banks of the river Amstel.

They were also able to build a bridge that connected to a huge saltwater inlet where they can fish for herring among other things. The dams mainly protected the small fishing community from regular rise of the river IJ. If not then the community will get flooded every time the tide goes up.

The settlement itself was perfectly established especially for trade. The mouth of the Amstel River basically formed a rather natural harbor. Small trading ships that can travel deeper inland made their way easily into this harbor. Larger Koggeships came with their huge supply of goods to exchange and barter, bringing with them much-needed items.

Recent archaeological digs confirm that there were other people who settled in the rich area of the Amstel long before the fishing village was established. Archaeologists found pottery, pole axes, and other artifacts that dated all the way back to the New Stone Age. This means that human beings and other communities may have come and gone in the area since around 2600 BCE.

From the 12th century on, early Amsterdam increasingly became a center of trade. The beer trade strengthened commerce coming in and out of the city. Trade ties with other cities and territories in the Baltic Sea and the Hanseatic League were formed. And, during the 15th century, Amsterdam eventually became the central granary of sorts. Grains that were to be traded or transported to what was then known as the low countries of the north came from Amsterdam. The city quickly became the most important trading city in all of Holland.

Historical Trivia
Revolution and Independence
There were many reasons why the Dutch revolted against

Spain. One reason, of course, was religious intolerance. Another reason was political since there was very little power granted to the local nobility. The rebellion began in 1578, and it came to be known as the Eighty Years' War. The revolt of the people eventually led to Dutch independence.

Amsterdam along with the other Dutch cities became quite tolerant. People believed whatever they wanted as long as it is within certain limits. Many sought refuge in the Dutch Republic while religious wars raged throughout Europe at the time. This paradigm of tolerance and acceptance remains today an important hallmark of Amsterdam.

The Golden Age and Modernization

The years following the Dutch independence were known as the Golden Age. Amsterdam back then gave the largest amounts of taxes compared to the other states in the country. Trade and commerce was on the rise and city's population reached its peak at 200,000.

The government was able to provide well for their constituents. A lot of essential care was provided in the form of hospitals, almshouses, churches, as well as houses for the elderly.

Eventually, the city went into a decline. The city was ravaged by the Bubonic Plague from 1663 to 1666, which should be expected from a trading hub. More than 10% of the city's population died. A lot of the rich folks closed their shops and businesses and left. The many wars of the Dutch Republic with other countries also ushered in the city's decline. World Wars I and II also contributed largely to the losses in Amsterdam.

The Jewish community was deported, which included Anne Frank. Along with their leaving was the demise of the city's diamond trade. All of the investors in the prestigious Amsterdam diamond industry were Jews.

The years 1940 to the present represented the years of recovery. The city's economy switched from industrial to that of a service economy. Economic recessions have come and gone. The city today has become one of the popular tourist destinations in the world.

29

Transport

Transport Options

Amsterdam is one of the most visited cities in Europe. That means there are a lot of transport options to get into the city. You can actually get to it by land, sea, and air. There are also a lot of cheap flights from Europe, which should be your number one option. The Schiphol Airport in Amsterdam is one of the largest and busiest airports in the world. It's the fourth largest airport in all of Europe.

Schiphol Airport Website

Schiphol Airport Map

Getting Around the City

Once you're in Amsterdam, there are a lot of different ways to get around from one point of interest to the other. The following are many different means of transport that you can use to get to the places you want to visit. Note that some means of transport will cost more than others.

Riding on a Bike

If you really want to travel like the Dutch people do then you better hop on a bicycle. Cycling is a way of life for the locals and this is one of the best ways to immerse yourself in the local culture. There are bike paths all over Amsterdam so don't worry about sharing the road with cars, trucks, buses, and all the other vehicles that ply the streets. There are lots of bicycle rental companies in the city and they usually charge a rental fee of eight euros.

Bike Rental Map

City Taxis

Taxis are more expensive than other means of transport in Amsterdam. Taxi rates begin at €1.80 per kilometer and there is also a 5 to 10 percent tip (optional). Convenience definitely comes with a price. You'll find most taxis within the tourist hubs and their service is prompt. However, note that getting one during the weekends will be a bit difficult.

Bike Taxis

So there are regular taxis and there are bicycles – the most common travel options in town; but now you can also hop on bike taxis – a combination of bicycles and taxis. It's like a gondola that's been given a modern twist. You can call it the environmentally friendly revolution.

The downside is that these things can only take two passengers at a time. It doesn't pollute the air and it doesn't make any loud noises. It squeaks from time to time and the driver has to ring the bell from time to time. These three-wheeled pedal powered taxis also come with batteries – adds extra power in case the driver takes an extra heavy passenger or when the road takes on an extra high slope. You pay 1 euro for every 3 minutes of the ride.

Trams, Trains, and Buses

Trams are considered as the best ways to go around the city. Trams will be rolling around until 12:15 am. Another option is the Amsterdam Metro System. All trips start at the Central Station. Trains are the more convenient way to travel in case you're leaving Amsterdam. If you want to reach many of the suburbs then hop on a bus. Night buses are also your option when trams have stopped running. Night bus trips start at 12:30 am and end at 7 in the morning.

Transport Website

Rent a Car

Renting a car in Amsterdam and driving in the city is not recommended for tourists. The roads can be pretty difficult to maneuver and finding a place to park will be quite a hassle. But if you insist on driving, then you can find car rentals right at the airport and in the city center.

30

Hotels

Amsterdam can be expensive, but I have made a short list of budget hotels that might be a good fit for you:

Citizenm Hotel

This lovely boutique hotel is modern with fantastic service.What makes this hotel even better is the affordable prices.This is a very good deal for a budget traveler who want to stay in a nice hotel with modern features and a nice location away from the city noise.

Phone:+31(0)208117080

citizenM Amsterdam

Prinses Irenestraat 30

1077 WX Amsterdam

Citizenm Hotel Website

Hotel Brouwer

If you want to stay in the center of Amsterdam and be walking distance from most things in Amsterdam, then get a room at the Hotel Brouwer.The hotel is located next to a canal and is one of the best locations in Amsterdam.

Phone:31-(0)20-624-6358

Singel 83

1012 VE Amsterdam

Hotel Brouwer Website

Between Art and Kitsch b&b Amsterdam

In true Amsterdam style, this hotel is something different than your normal bed and breakfast hotel.It's difficult to describe this hotel, except to say that its a mix of old, new and eccentric.If you are looking for something different then this for you.

Phone:+31 20 6790485

Ruysdaelkade 75-2

1072 AL Amsterdam

Between Art and Kitsch b&b Website

Seven Bridges Hotel
The Seven Bridges is a 300-year-old hotel located in the heart of Amsterdam. The name says seven bridges, and that is what you get. The hotel has a view over seven bridges on the canal and is a classic place to stay for your short stay.
Phone: + 31-20-6231329
Seven Bridges Hotel
Reguliersgracht 31
1017 LK Amsterdam

Seven Bridges Hotel Website

Click Here for more Amsterdam Hotel Options

31

Amsterdam's Best Museums

There are a lot of reasons why Amsterdam is named as the world's 2nd best city to live in. Other than its rich history, the place also has a lot of interesting attractions. Included in this huge list of attractions is a plethora of museums. Statistics show that the city of Amsterdam has more museums than any other city in the world per square meter. That includes a lot of historical buildings that house many cultural treasures, artifacts, and art.

The following is a list of some of the most popular and important museums in Amsterdam. The list also includes a few interesting museums that don't get noticed as much as the more prominent ones.

Rijksmuseum

Rijksmuseum is the most popular museum in the city. It's actually the most popular museum in the Netherlands – well, they won't call it the Dutch national museum for nothing. It had a really huge facelift beginning in 2003. The renovation and modernization work took about ten years to complete. It was reopened to the public in April 13, 2013. The Rijksmuseum showcases the best in Dutch art. It houses some of the most important historical artifacts in the country. It also has an extensive collection of Asian and European art.

Rijksmuseum is located at Museumstraat 1, the Museum Quarter. The place is open from 9 am to 5 pm.

Website

Rijksmuseum Map

The Cheese Museum

One of the really popular museums in Amsterdam is the House of Anne Frank. People visit the place for its huge historical value. However, right across the street from the famed Anne Frank House is another interesting place, though it is not as celebrated as the museum right in front of it.

You may not even notice the Cheese Museum since it looks like a regular café or snack bar. Nevertheless, this museum has been keeping alive a tradition that has been around for centuries. The cheese industry in Netherlands has about 600 years in its history. That history as well as the many different flavors of unique cheeses is preserved and highlighted in this museum.

So, who will be interested to visit such an odd museum? It's the food lovers, of course. Seeing row upon row of different cheeses with their own unique flavors is enough to make a foodie's heart leap twice. Of course, you can sample the different cheeses to your heart's content.

The Cheese Museum is located at Prinsensgracht 112, 1015 EA, Amsterdam. Admission is only one Euro. The place is open to visitors from 10 in the morning to 6 in the evening. The only downside to the place is that they don't have much space. That means they can't accommodate a large crowd of visitors. Website

Cheese Museum Map

Van Gogh Museum

This is one of the more prestigious museums in the world.

Mention the name Van Gogh and people almost instantly know who's being referred to. Obviously, the collection you'll find in this museum will be the works Vincent van Gogh. It also contains the works of other 19th century artists.

Another treasure trove in this museum is the collected letters of Van Gogh to his colleagues and family. They especially reveal his feelings toward his art and it gives us a window to look into the soul and inner workings of this one of a kind artist.

The museum is located within the Museum Quarter, so it won't be that hard to find. Its entrance is located at Paulus Potterstraat 7. The museum is usually open from 9 am to 6 pm. They also have different events scheduled every Friday.
Website

Van Gogh Museum Map

Stedelijk Museum

Stedelijk is the municipal museum of Amsterdam. It's dedicated to modern art – unlike the other collections you'll find elsewhere. It was established in the year 1895. It initially housed collections of different art works and historical items. It was only during the 1970's when this museum became dedicated to modern art.

The museum has undergone extensive renovation. Today it sports a more modern feel to it. Well, basically the design of the interior matches the type of collection it currently holds.

Every now and then the museum also hosts lectures, concerts, films, and other performances, which is a treat in case you happen to be there for a special event.

The Stedelijk is open daily from 10 am to 6 pm. However, they open from 11 am to 10 pm on Thursdays. You'll find the entrance at Museumplein 10, Amsterdam.

Website

Stedelijk Museum Map

Anne Frank House

The Anne Frank house is one of the really popular places to visit in Amsterdam. It's a solemn place that breathes the grim history of World War II. It literally attracts throngs of people;

and unfortunately, you have to line up just to get a glimpse of the place where the Frank family and others hid from Nazi army.

The interior of the house is hollow and empty now. Yet in these quiet quarters lay the silent testimony of the people who lived there. Visitors will find actual items that belonged to the people who lived there. Anne Frank's original diary is on display along with her other notes. Some quotes from her writings are also on display.

The one hour tour will include a view of pretty much everything. A virtual tour will allow you to see the entire place. It will also provide visitors with a lot of background information. Note that the museum doesn't have facilities for people with disabilities. Remember, this is where people hid, so don't expect it to have wide open spaces.

Expect really long lines during summer. If you want to avoid the really long snaking lines of visitors from all over the world, then schedule your visit to the Anne Frank House from March to October. The museum is usually open from 9 am to 9 pm. The museum is located at Prinsengracht 267, 1016 GV, Amsterdam.

Website

Anne Frank House Map

The Museum of Prostitution

No visit to Amsterdam will be complete without a visit to one of the erotic museums there. The Museum of Prostitution is one of the best ones you will find. Now, this is one museum that isn't exactly child-friendly. You should leave the kids at home if you're planning to visit this place. It's situated perfectly right in the middle of Amsterdam's red light district, in Binnenstad. It's pretty hard to miss. The tour of the place isn't going to last you an hour and the whole exhibition will cost you less than 10 euros.

You'll be treated to a short discourse on the history of prostitution in Amsterdam. It will also give you a first person point of view of what it's like to be behind the windows with the red lights. You'll learn first-hand what it feels like to be the girl sitting inside the glass casement, as it were.

An interesting part of the visit to this museum is the tour of the various chambers where the prostitutes perform their profession. The various implements and props will be explained to you and you'll have a lot of photo ops while you're in there. You can see it as a chance to be educated about the ins and outs of this one of a kind profession. Some people will come out displeased of course but there are those who will experience a small paradigm shift after the tour – how each person reacts is simply a subjective experience.

Website

Museum of Prostitution Map

Science Center Nemo

This is one of the museums that will amaze young children. The place offers a lot of attractions that highlight the wonders of science while providing kids a lot of entertainment. Children can take part in many different experiments and understand just how the world works.

They'll have fun creating gigantic soap bubbles, figuring out how electronic gadgets work, and explore the mysteries of physics and chemistry. They'll learn the many characteristics of sound and visual media as well. The building itself is absolutely interesting – imagine walking into the very hull of a huge ship.

The Science Center Nemo is usually crowded from May to August, which is its peak season. The low season is from September to April. You'll find it on Oosterdok 2, 1011 VX

Amsterdam. They're open from 10 am to 5:30 pm.

Website

Science Center Nemo Map

National Maritime Museum

The National Maritime Museum, or locally known as the Het Scheepvaartmuseum, is also another interesting place for kids and adults. Much of the collections you'll find in this museum includes maritime artifacts – well, Amsterdam began as a fishing village and it was a center of trade with a natural port at one time in its history. Maritime travels and business is a big part of the history of the city.

There are exhibits that are specially tailored for kids such as Sal and Yori and Circus Sea, My Expo, and the Tale of the Whale.

The other exhibits are quite informational such as Navigational Instruments, Port 24/7, and See You in The Golden Age. There are sections of the museum where kids can play video games, view multimedia presentations, and other attractions that allow kids to learn and play.

The National Maritime Museum is open daily from 9 am to 5 pm. The museum will be closed on certain holidays. You can find the museum in Kattenburgerplein 1, 1018 KK Amsterdam.

Website

National Maritime Museum Map

32

Best Art Galleries

The previous chapter enumerated some of the best museums that you can find in Amsterdam and in the Netherlands. Notice that a lot of these museums feature classic and contemporary artworks. Some of these important museums include the Stadsarchief (or the City Archive) which is full of Art Deco murals; Verzetsmuseum (the Museum of the Resistance) which features life in Amsterdam under Nazi Germany; Jewish Historical Museum which features Jewish art and the city's Jewish history; and the Hermitage Amsterdam that showcases collections that are on loan from the Hermitage Palace (St. Petersburg).

This book is focused on the short stay traveller, but I have included links and maps to the above-mentioned museums if you do have extra time to visit them.

Stadsarchief Website

Stadsarchief Map

Verzetsmuseum Website

Verzetsmuseum Map

Jewish Historical Museum Website

Jewish Historical Museum Map

Hermitage Amsterdam Website

Hermitage Amsterdam Map

The following are some of the interesting art galleries in the city. Some of them take on a particular theme. There are plenty of these galleries where visitors can admire the art and also purchase some of the items that are on display.

Contemporary and Modern Art

If you're interested in taking home some of the best in contemporary art then just walk around the shopping district. You'll find a gallery in just about every block. For instance, the ArTicKs Gallery located on Singel 88 features the best in steel art. Their collections include works from different genres including punk, low brow, comic, stencil, and graffiti. The KochxBos Gallery on the other hand features the works of some of the brightest talents from various parts of the world. You'll find it on Anjeliersdwarsstraat 36.

ArTicKs Gallery Map

The KochxBos Gallery Map

Other galleries that feature modern and contemporary art include the Akinci Gallery in Lijnbaansgracht 317 1017 WZ Amsterdam; Arti et Amicitiae with an official address in Rokin 112, 1012 LB Amsterdam; and Bart, Galerie Amsterdam, which features the best and brightest of Amsterdam's artists. Bart is located in Bloemgracht 2, 1015TH Amsterdam.

Akinci Gallery Map

Arti et Amicitiae Map

Bart Galerie Amsterdam Map

Now let's take a look at the galleries you should definitely visit in Amsterdam.

Torch Gallery

Established in 1984, Torch is one of the newer yet more popular art galleries in Amsterdam. It specializes in new media as well as photography. Much of the works on display take on a rather experimental theme. You can even say that the artists featured here take on rather bold strokes using new media as their paint brush. The gallery's current address is Lauriergracht 94, 1016 RN Amsterdam.

Website

Torch Gallery Map

Galerie Lieve Hemel

Galerie Lieve Hemel is the go to place for people who want to stick with purely realistic paintings. The collections mainly include works from Dutch artists. This art gallery is currently located at Nieuwe Spiegelstraat 3, 1017 DB Amsterdam having moved from its former address.

Website

Galerie Lieve Hemel

Jaski Art Gallery

Have you ever heard of the CoBrA abstract movement? You'll find an extensive collection of art from that genre here in the Jaski Art Gallery. This gallery is the dream child of former tennis champion Tom Okker. The gallery's address is Nieuwe Spiegelstraat 29, 1017 DB Amsterdam.

Website

Jaski Art Gallery Map

Gerhard Hofland Gallery

Gerhard Hofland Gallery is one of the more ambitious galleries in Amsterdam. They feature some of the best artists in the Netherlands and Germany. The exhibits are often described as both striking and surprising. Needless to say, the artists and the gallery owner are striving hard to get museum recognition. The address of this art gallery is Bilderdijkstraat 165c, 1053 KP, Amsterdam.

Website

Gerhard Hofland Gallery Map

Carla Koch, Gallery

This gallery features the works of Carla Koch. The collection includes works that center on glass and ceramics as the primary medium. You'll find the gallery in Veemkade 500 (6th floor), building Detroit, 1019 HE Amsterdam.

Website

Carla Koch, Gallery Map

Braggiotti Gallery

This art gallery mainly features glass art. It also highlights the best from local artists as well as works from artists from other countries. You'll find the gallery in Singel 424, 1016 AK Amsterdam.

Website

Braggiotti Gallery Map

33

A Potpourri of Flavors from Amsterdam's Restaurants

Amsterdam hasn't made its mark in the culinary world, yet. However, restaurants dot the city – and a good number of them have earned their very own Michelin stars. You'll find a mixture of culinary backgrounds and potpourri of different cuisines. It's definitely a place where good old homey Dutch cooking meets and greets the rest of the world. At times, you'll find a fusion as chefs, and everybody else manning the kitchen tries to outdo the other restaurant when coming up with something new.

The following is a short list of restaurants that serve the general public in Amsterdam. Note that some are pricier than others. The list also includes some interesting but not so popular restaurants.

Blue Spoon
Blue Spoon is the go-to place for the hungry guests who have booked rooms in the Andaz Hotel. They offer Dutch food

with a bit of a French flair – or is it the other way around? Well anyway, it doesn't really matter because when the waiters walk by with a huge platter of food in hand, the flavorful aroma wafting in the air will be enough to make you forget which cuisine you're sampling.

If you're a fan of minimalist design, then the décor here won't disappoint. There is a touch of elegance in the simplicity of the ambiance in this place. You'll find Blue Spoon at Andaz Prinsengracht Hotel, Prinsengracht 587, 1016 HT. Meal prices here range from €40 to €45.

Website

Blue Spoon Map

Mamouche

If you haven't tried Moroccan cuisine, then allow Mamouche to give you that well-deserved first taste. You can say that the flavors of the food here are slightly out of this world. Imagine the ingredients – oysters, scallops, tuna, orange dressing, figs, avocadoes, and goat's cheese.

The feel of the place is rather warm yet friendly. Diners also have the option to dine a la carte. Considering the neighborhood it's in (i.e. De Pijp) expect young professionals to gather here at lunch time and after working hours. You'll find this restaurant at Quellijnstraat 104, 1072 XZ. Meal prices here average at €40.

Website

Mamouche Map

Wink

Judging by the name of this restaurant, you can tell that it's playful and cheery. The red table tops actually add to that overall feel. It's a relatively small restaurant, and you may even be tempted to call it your mom's home kitchen. However, the chef working behind the scenes actually whip up miracles in their little hatch. It's one of those places where you can allow your taste buds to experience the very best of Dutch cooking mixed and matched with the best that pure talent can concoct.

You can find Wink at Govert Flinckstraat 326, 1073 CJ, which is easily accessible via Tram 4. They are open from Tuesdays to Saturdays from 6 in the evening to 10 pm. Food prices here average at 35 euros.

Website

Wink Map

Serre

If formal dining is just too formal or if the food prices in fancy restaurants are just too high then you may want to tone things down a little at Serre. The place is definitely elegant, but it doesn't carry a lot of flair. You still get a great fine dining experience minus the crazy prices that may cut travel budget a bit short. Now, even though everything is scaled down at Serre, they still offer the classic Bibendum Menu, and the canal terrace provides an ecstatic view minus the usual rumble of city traffic you get from other places. This restaurant is at Hotel Okura, Ferdinand Bolstraat 333, 1072 LH. Meal prices average at 36 euros.

Website

Serre Map

De Reiger

Care to dine in the old Amsterdam way? Then look for De Reiger since they offer pretty much that kind of dining experience. The menu here changes on a daily basis. Each day you'll be treated to a different set of flavors that only the Dutch can provide. The restaurant has preserved the ambiance of the good old days when that part of the city's quarter was reserved for the working class. The old prints are still up on the walls, and the deco lamps still bring back the feel of bygone decades.

Here's a quick tip – make sure to come early. Nevertheless, even though a line usually forms, the wait time isn't that long. You can find this restaurant at Nieuwe Leliestraat 34, 1015 ST. They are open from noon to 10:30 pm. Meal prices average at 38 euros.

Website

De Reiger Map

Wing Kee

If you're hungry for some Chinese food, then don't forget that wherever you go in the world, you will always find some sort of a China Town or a Chinese quarter. Now, not all Chinese food is the same, and some these restaurants have a certain specialties. Wing Kee is the sort of restaurant that serves really succulent food in generous servings.

You just have to try their roasted suckling pig – it's crispy and crackling. The meat is cooked to perfection – it's so tender it melts in your mouth. If you're not into eating a lot of pork, then you ought to at least try their roasted duck. Just like your traditional Chinese restaurant, you can find the roasted ducks hanging by the window, cooked golden brown succulently roasted.

Website

Wing Lee Map

Japan Inn

Can't have enough of authentic Asian food? Then try the food from Japan Inn. The décor and mood of the place is rather modest. The tamed lighting matches the low key interiors quite nicely. Of course, they serve the best of Japanese cuisine. Of course, this is one of the places in the city Japanese expats and students find their way after a long day at work or school.

You'll find Japan Inn at Leidsekruisstraat 4, 1017 RH. They're open from 5:30 pm to 11:30 pm. Meal prices here average at €22.

Website

Japan Inn Map

Moeders

If you're in Amsterdam, then you ought to at least sample the authentic Dutch cuisine. If that's the type of flavor you want to get, then sample the food served in Moeders (translated as "mothers"). The walls of this restaurant are covered with pictures of mothers – the meals, of course, are cooked just the way Dutch moms would cook them.

If you want to sample all the food on the menu then order a sampler – it will have pretty much all the stuff you'll find on the menu. That way you get to sample the best of the local cuisine in one go. Moeders is located at Rozengracht 251, 1016 SX Amsterdam.

Website

Moeders Map

Beddington's

In case you have the cash to burn, and you really want to

try one of the best high-end restaurants in Amsterdam then try the food served in Beddington's. The restaurant has been around since 1983. The food served here is a fusion of Asian, English, and Dutch cuisine. You'll be treated to the best of Derbyshire home cooking with all the twists and turns to delight your taste buds. Meal prices here range from €48 to €55. They restaurant is open from Tuesdays to Saturdays from 7 pm onwards.

Website

Beddington's Map

Restaurant Greetje

Restaurant Greetje takes Dutch cuisine and then takes it to a whole new level. Just try their stamppot; it tastes like the traditional dish but with a gleeful flavor added to it. The secret, of course, is to replace some of the ingredients to make a subtle twist in the flavor. The food is also plated to perfection. You can find this restaurant at Peperstraat 23-25. Meal prices start at €25. They're open from Sundays, and Tuesdays to Fridays from 6 to 10 in the evening. On Saturdays, they open from 6 to 11 in the evening.

Website

Restaurant Greetje Map

Razmataz

Razmataz is one of the few restaurants in Amsterdam that stays open from breakfast to dinner. The meals served here are mainly Mediterranean and French. Note that the menu changes with the season. The crowd that usually gathers here mainly includes the younger generation. They start coming in for a bit of morning coffee. In the evening, the guests stay a little longer for some after dinner drinks. You can find this restaurant at Hugo de Grootplein 7. Food prices here start at 20 euros. They're usually open from 8:30 am to 1 am. On some days, they open at 9 in the morning.

Website

Razmataz Map

34

Shopping

Shopping in Amsterdam

Another thing that makes Amsterdam a popular tourist destination shopping. Visitors come here to shop for just about anything. Here you will find curious items, antiques, trinkets, strange souvenirs, and even diamonds. Shopping centers usually open at 9 in the morning and close at 6 in the evening. However, there are many late night shopping centers too, and they usually close at 9 pm.

The Shopping Neighborhoods

There are many streets and neighborhoods in Amsterdam that are lined with shops and boutiques. Close to the Central Station you'll immediately be greeted by a kilometer long shopping district from Nieuwedijk to Kalverstraat. There is no road traffic, so all you'll see are pedestrians, tourists, students, and other folks from different walks of life. The entire stretch of road is lined with shops and stalls displaying their wares.

If you're looking for gift items, bags, and other accessories then try the stores at Kalverstraat. They also have ice cream stores and restaurants in case you get hungry. On the same road, you'll also find the flower market. There you can find the world famous bulbs and tulips that you can take home with you. If you're looking for more signature items, then head out to the Oud Zuid district where you'll find shops with names like Gucci, Tommy Hilfiger, Cartier, and others.

Nieuwedijk Map

Kalverstraat Map

Kalverstraat Website

Oud Zuid District Map

Malls and Department Stores

Of course, there are also malls and department stores in the city. You'll find a lot of the imported stuff in these places. One of the most popular department stores is De Bijenkorf. If you want to see pretty much every mall in the city then walk on to the Dam square. The only mall that isn't on that square is Villa Arena.

De Bijenkorf Map

Dam Square Map

Let's take a lot at some of the best and unique stores in Amsterdam:

The American Book Center

This store has a very big variety of books of many different genres.The store has three floors and hosts a variety of events like book signings, meeting with authors and conferences.This store also has a wide variety of English magazines.

The store is open every day:
Monday, Tue, Wed, Fri, Sat: 10am – 8pm
Thurs: 10am – 9pm
Sun: 11am – 6pm

Website

The American Book Center Map

Iittala

The Dutch are famous for their love of design.The character of the Dutch design is minimalist, experimental and innovative.So these days the Dutch has fell in love with this store from Finland that is known for their excellent designs.This Finnish design brand specializes in design objects, tableware, and cookware.

Mon: 12:00pm - 6:00pm
Tue: Wed, Fri 10:00am - 6:00pm
Thu: 10:00am - 9:00pm
Sat: 10:00am - 6:00pm
Sun :12:00pm - 6:00pm

Website

Map

HEMA

HEMA is a very popular chain of department stores all over the Netherlands.The interesting thing about HEMA is that they design and produce everything they sell.A Hema you will find almost anything you want, and you will have a unique Dutch shopping experience.

Mon - Wed:09:00am - 07:00pm
Thurs: 09:00am - 09:00pm
Fri - Sat: 09:00am -07:00pm
Sun: 12:00am - 06:00pm

Website

HEMA Map

Droog

Droog is probably one of the most interesting stores you will visit in Amsterdam.They are famous for cutting edge design and products.Droog uses unlikely or discarded materials and turns them into amazing products.
Tue - Sun 11:00am - 18:00pm
Mon -Closed

Website

Droog Map

If you're interested in shopping for antiques, then your best shot is to look for antique shops in the city's shopping market. There you'll find food, clothing items, some fixtures, and antiques. The markets are only a short walk away from the city center.

I have made a list of the top markets and vintage stores:

De Looier Arts & Antiques

This place might not look it from the outside, but its the largest and most popular antique market in the Netherlands.You can find almost anything in this big treasure chest.This store has anything from old watches to old paintings.This is one of my favorite markets in Amsterdam, and you will leave with something special.

-Elandsgracht 109, 1016 TT Amsterdam
The store is not open every day:
Mon,Wed,Thu,Fi : 10am - 6pm
Tue: Closed
Sat ,Sun :10am - 5pm

De Looier Arts & Antiques Map

Wini Vintage

If you are into vintage clothing, then look no further than Wini.You will find good quality vintage clothing and at a reasonable price.The main focus in this store is for women, but they have a small collection of vintage men's clothing.

-Haarlemmerstraat 29, 1013 EJ Amsterdam
Wini is Open every day:
Mon - Wed: 10:30am - 6:00pm
Thurs 10:30am - 6.30pm
Fri and Sat: 10:30am - 6:00pm
Sun: 12.00pm - 6:00pm
Website

Wini Vintage Map

Waterlooplein Markt
Waterlooplein is the most popular flea market in Amster-

dam and many tourist flocks here to get to the best goods first.This is a great place to find a bargain and negotiate a good price.Stand your ground with some of the pushy sellers and make sure you get a reasonable price.On Saturdays, the market turns into organic farmers heaven.

 -Waterlooplein 2, Amsterdam
 Mon - Fri: 09:00am - 05:30pm
 Sat: 8:30am - 5:30pm
 Website

 Waterlooplein Markt Map

Noordermarkt

This amazing open-air market is a great place to visit if you like great food and vintage goods.The combination of the two is awesome and its a great to shop while snacking on some Dutch cheese.All the organic farmers in the Netherlands bring their goods to be sold hear.If you are in Amsterdam on a Monday, then drop into Noordermarkt because they market will sell a wide variety of antique goods, ranging from clothes to books.

Opening Times:
Mon: 9:00am - 2:00pm
Sat 9:00am - 4:00pm
Website

Noordermarkt Map

35

Cafe's (coffee)

When you're in Amsterdam, you should remember that there is a difference between a café and a coffee shop. A café is where you get your coffee and snacks, but a coffee shop is something else. Yes, it's one of those places where you can legally smoke marijuana, and other kinds of soft drugs. We'll deal with those places later in this book.

For now, you'll find some of the best places to get your coffee in the list below:

Café Het Paleis
This café is conveniently located near Dam square, where many of the tourist sites and places of interest are located. It's a great place to take a break, have a beer or a cup of coffee along with some pastries before heading out to your next destination. Try their apple tarts and sandwiches. You'll find it at Paleisstraat 16.

Website

Café Het Paleis Map

Pannenkoekenhuis Upstairs

Aside from the coffee, Pannenkoekenhuis serves some of the best treats to help you get through a hangover. Their Dutch pancakes are their signature treats. The food is a bit pricey but the location is great – nothing like fresh air to set things straight. You'll find this café at Grimburgwal 2.

Website

Pannenkoekenhuis Upstairs Map

Poco Loco

You can come to Poco Loco for your morning coffee to start your day. You can also return to the place to cap off your night with some of the best local beer. You should also try their tapas just to go with your drinks. Expect this café to be a bit crowded – it's that popular. You'll find it at Nieuwmarkt 24.

Website

Poco Loco Map

Singel 404

You should avoid this café during lunch time. It is usually packed with students lining up for a meal. Well, sometimes they bring more tables out, which gives you a good view of the canal but even then, if you come in late you may have to wait a while to get a seat. Afternoons here are less crowded. They even serve a good brew of coffee with some cake to match your mood.

Website

Singel 404 Map

36

Bars and Clubs

Amsterdam has an awesome nightlife, and you will find great places to have fun if you have a lot of time to explore the city.The problem is you probably won't have the time to walk around Amsterdam hoping you find the right place.So I made a list of the best bars and clubs for you to consider.

The Tara

The Tara use to be an English Pub, but these days its has a real Amsterdam flavour mixed with the concepts of a traditional British pub.It is modern, cosy, and the food is good.If you are looking for good beer in a warm and cosy atmosphere, then visit the Tara.The Tara shows popular sports events and has live music on some evenings.The Tara has three bars, seven rooms and two sidewalk terraces.

Opening Times: Monday to Sunday 10 am - 1 am
Website

The Tara Map

Brouwerij 't IJ

This is a special location in Amsterdam.Firstly it's located in an old Windmill, and secondly it's one of the best micro-breweries in the city.This bar has an amazing collection of high-quality beers.If you visit one bar in Amsterdam, then visit the Brouwerij IJ.

Open Daily from 2 pm - 8 pm
Website

Brouwerij 't IJ Map

Hanneke's Boom

This place looks more like an old beach house than a bar and it's built right next to water.Hanneke's Boom is one of the most popular hangouts in Amsterdam and is built and decorated with second-hand items.In the summer, the locals visit the bar by boat and it gets crowded.Great spot for a cold beer in the summer.This place is over 300 years old so visit this unique spot.Come by boat or on foot.

Website

Hanneke's Boom Map

Whiskycafé L&B

Whiskycafé L&B stock around 1400 different types of Whisky and Bourbon from around the world.The staff at this bar are very knowledgeable about whisky, so you will easily be pointed in the right direction if the large selection becomes overwhelming.This bar is very relaxed but has a nice and warm atmosphere.

Opening Times:
Sun – Thurs 8 pm – 3 am
Fri – Sat 8pm – 4 am

Website

Whiskycafé L&B Map

De Zotte

Belgian beer lovers usually find their way to De Zotte. You can find several good brews here for you to sample. Don't forget to get either grilled lamb or steak to go with your drink. You'll find this bar and café at Raamstraat 29.

Opening times:
Mon – Thurs 4pm –1am
Fri – Sat 2pm – 3am
Website

De Zotte Map

Van Kerkwijk

At first glance, you might think that this café is nothing more than shady back alley beer pub south of the Dam square. Well, that's what you'll get when you look at the place from the outside. Walk in and you'll find it buzzing with life. This café is quite popular with its rather rustic menu. Most of the meals have a rather French twist but the steaks are godly well-seasoned – something that will make you come back again and again. You'll find the place at Nes 41.

Opening Times:
Open Daily from 11am - 1am
Website

Van Kerkwijk Map

Getto

Getto is the place where you can get great cocktails and great burgers. Each burger on the menu is named after a drag queen that performs there. Check out their website to find out who is performing. You'll find this one of a kind bar and café at Warmoesstraat.

Opening Times:
Sun 4:30pm: - 12:00am
Tues , Wed , Thurs 4:30pm -1:00am
Fri 4:30pm - 2:00am
Website

Getto Map

Studio 80

Although this is kind of a hipster hangout, it is a one of the best clubs in Amsterdam.The DJ's at the club are great, and they focus on a type of minimal techno music.This is one of the trendiest clubs in Amsterdam, and you should expect to see the weird and wonderful of Amsterdam making their appearance.So if you have an open mind then visit Studio 80.

Website

Studio 80 Map

Bitterzoet

If you are not into techno and you are looking for something more laid back, then this is the club for you.A good way to describe Bitterroot's sound is that it's a mix between urban, jazz and soul.This club has a dark and sexy feeling to it.Friday's in Bitterzoet is funk and soul night, so if that's your thing then pop into the club.

Website

Bitterzoet Map

Sugar Factory

Sugar Factory is one of the unique clubs in Amsterdam where performance and clubbing meet and creates something you will only find in Amsterdam.The club used to be a theatre, and a large stage is right next to the dance floor where a variety of performance clubbing happens while the club is in full steam.Think of Sugar Factory as a Dynamic playground for the open-minded.

Website

Sugar Factory Map

Jimmy Woo

This is the place to be seen in Amsterdam.If you want to be surrounded by Dutch Supermodels and Celebrities, then go to Jimmy Woo.The club has a dark smokey atmosphere and plays a mix of Hip Hop and House Music.

Website

Jimmy Woo Map

37

Only in Amsterdam

Only in Amsterdam

Each place on earth has something unique to offer. Just like many of the popular touristy places in the world, Amsterdam has many unique offerings. In this chapter you'll find some of the things that you can only find in this city.

Coffee Shops

There's no better way to say it than just to be candid about it and just say it. One of the reasons why some people visit Amsterdam is to try the coffee shops. Coffee shops in this city, as you know, are not little snack bars that serve nice smelling hot coffee. It's a place where they sell soft drugs, marijuana, and cannabis.

Mentioning that in this book doesn't mean that the author condones or promotes the use of controlled substances. Nevertheless, these shops are unique to Amsterdam and spending some time smoking pot here is one of the truly unique things that people can do when they visit the city.

I made a list of the best coffee shops in Amsterdam for those of you considering to visit a coffee shop.

Barney's Coffeeshop

What makes this place special?Well, it's located in a 500-year-old building.This shops has won a few high times awards and serves great food.

Open Daily from 7am - 10pm
-Haarlemmerstraat 102, 1013 EW Amsterdam
Website

Barney's Coffeeshop Map

Bluebird

Bluebird was founded in 1982 and is nearby the red light district.The food at Bluebird is excellent, and the staff speaks English well.

Open Daily from 9 am - 1:30 am
-Sint Antoniesbreestraat 71, 1011 HB Amsterdam
Bluebird Map

The Bulldog

Everybody in Amsterdam knows about the Bulldog.If you think about Amsterdam Coffee Shops, then you think the Bulldog.The Bulldog was the first coffee shop in Amsterdam, and the original Bulldog is located in a former Amsterdam Police Station.There are now a few new Bulldog shops around, but I recommend you visit the original shop in Leidseplein 15.

The Bulldog is open daily from 10am-1am
-Leidseplein 15, 1017 PS Amsterdam
Website

The Bulldog Map

Smoke Palace

If you want to have a coffee shop experience away from the crowds in a very relaxed setting, then visit Smoke Palace.Smoke Place is located in the eastern district of Amsterdam.

Open Daily from 9 am -1 am
-Linnaeusstraat 83 HS, 1093 EK Amsterdam

Website

Smoke Palace Map

Smart Shops

Smart shops in Amsterdam are pretty much the same as coffee shops – with a slight difference of course. Smart shops, just like coffee shops, sell soft drugs, but they only sell smart drugs (i.e. the ones that stimulate the brain to improve memory and cognitive functions).

You can imagine students flocking here whenever there are exams. Here you'll find herbal medicines that are touted to improve your brain's functions. Herbal products like magic mushrooms, Gingko Biloba, Cola nut, and Guarana among others.The first smart shop in Amsterdam was Kokopelli.

Kokopelli.

This is one of the 10 Smart Shops left in Amsterdam and it was also the first.They were the trendsetters with selling magic mushrooms after they started their business with energy drinks and herbs.

–Warmoesstraat 12, 1012 JD Amsterdam
Website

Kokopelli Map

Smart Shops Map

RED LIGHT DISTRICT

Amsterdam's Red Light District is another popular destination for many tourists. As you should know, prostitution is a legal profession in this city. Visitors have different reactions. Some come here with a sense of excitement, some look at the red fringed windows and stare in shock, while others giggle in a celebratory fashion. Now and then you will find busloads of tourists from different countries toting their beloved cameras – however, do take note that it is illegal to take pictures of the female entertainers. You'll find yourself and your camera in the wrong side of the law after that.

There are Red Light District tours if you are interested. You'll get lots of information about the place and one of the oldest industries in the world. Believe it or not, the RLD is actually one of the safest parts of Amsterdam. Security is pretty high with a lot of policemen on site. If you're planning to visit one of the brothels, peep shows, porno shows, and sex shops, you won't have to worry about getting robbed. Nevertheless, you should watch out for pickpockets since the streets tend to be quite crowded.

Red Light District Map

The Amsterdam Theaters Scene

Now, there's really more to Amsterdam than just drugs and sex. It's actually rich in history and culture. In fact, the place has a lively theater scene. Walk along Nes street stroll around the Leidseplein you'll find some of the best theaters in the city. Some of the performances are quite notable.

Website

Amsterdam and Art

They have the Van Gogh Museum and a plethora of other museums and art galleries that dot the city. Isn't that enough to convince you that art is a huge part of Dutch life and culture? Check out the addresses of the different art galleries and museums in the other chapters of this book.

Life in the Open Road

Bicycles are a staple in the lives of the people of Amsterdam. You can't say that you have truly mingled with the locals until you have tried their wheels. The bicycle scene gets even more interesting at night when the city lights come alive, and the many bridges get lighted. Start biking at Leidseplein and watch the city come alive as you get to Kerkstraat and the rest of Amsterdam.

Bicycle Website

Bicycle Rental Map

38

Sample 3 Day Itinerary

You can create your own 3 day itineraries given the places mentioned in this book. Of course, you will still need to work out some of the details like room and board reservations and transportation costs. You should buy a

Now, here's a sample three-day itinerary so you can have an idea how to set things up.

Day 1

9 am - 9 am - Rijksmuseum. Expect the place to be a bit crowded.

Tip: Get a map of the museum – it's pretty big. Spend three hours here.

Noon: Lunch time. Go to Go to Vondelpark and have lunch at Blauwe Theehuis. You'll stay here for about an hour or two.

2 pm - Van Gogh Museum

Tip: Get your ticket online and you can avoid the long queue of people by taking the priority line. The tour will take 2 to 3 hours.

5 pm – Museumplein – here you can watch the people play sports or better yet you can join in on the fun. It's a great place to meet the locals. You're stay here will take less than an hour.

6 pm –Canal Dinner Cruise – You will have dinner while on a boat cruise touring the city. The tour will last 3 hours and that will include dinner.

Day 2

9 am – Anne Frank House – take the tour, which will last about an hour or two.

11 am – Cheese Museum – Look around and enjoy the sight of many cheeses. You may even sample some of the cheeses if you like. The visit will last less than an hour.

Noon – Have lunch at the Jordaan – Take your pick and choose any of the many restaurants here. If you're not particularly hungry then grab a snack in one of the bars.

2 pm – Flower Market – Going to the flower market will be a bit of a stretch if you're on a bike. Nevertheless, the trip is worth it once you're at the flower market. You'll stay here for an hour.

Tip: If you want to take flowers home with you as souvenirs make sure to check the health inspection certificate of the flower packs before you buy them. The certification will tell you if the flower variant you're buying can be brought overseas.

3 pm – Go shopping – since you're already near

6 pm – Red Light District – roam around the Red Light District and enjoy the view. Try the services of the different shops if you want. There are bars and restaurants here where you can have your dinner.

Day 3

9 am – Science Center Nemo – this is a great place to bring the children along. Stay here for 1 to 3 hours

Noon – Lunch in Leiden Square at a restaurant of your choice. Stay here for 1 to 2 hours

2 pm –Albert Cuyp Market – Make sure to sample the Stroopwafels. Enjoy the frenzy of the market scene and look for a trinket that you can bring home with you. You may even find a piece of art that will inspire you. Shop here for 2 hours.

4 or 5 pm – Heineken – your Dutch experience won't be complete if you don't sample their beers and Heineken is the best place to get the best Dutch beer.

6 pm – Concertgebouw – enjoy the music at a live concert or watch a show in a theater if there is one. Make sure to try that distinct Dutch cultural experience while you're there.

8 pm – Bar hopping – it's your last night, better try some of the concoctions from one or two local bars.

For Guided Tours In Amsterdam CLICK HERE

39

EDINBURGH INTRODUCTION

Thank you for downloading the book "Edinburgh Travel Guide"

This book contains information about the charming city of Edinburgh, which is located in Scotland's Central Belt. This book will help you enjoy the unique attractions it has to offer. From castles steeped with a rich history to modern art galleries showcasing Scotland's high cultural society, the town is a serendipitous adventure waiting to happen.

Hailed as one of the most beautiful cities in Europe, Edinburgh is a town, which combines idyllic historical landmarks with the exciting and bustling cityscape environment. With so much to offer, it is Scotland's not so secret and widely popular holiday destination.

This guide features chapters dedicated to giving you all the information you need to have a splendid holiday in Scotland's capital city. Below are the chapters included in this book:

- About Edinburgh: A Brief History and Background
- Geographical and Weather Information
- The Best Time to Go: Holiday and Tourist Dates
- Top 5 Places to Stay at on a Budget
- Famous Landmarks That Shouldn't be Missed
- Getting Around: Edinburgh Transportation
- The Art Scene: Museums and Galleries to See
- The Gastronomic Scene: Restaurants and Coffee Shops
- Edinburg Night Life
- The Whiskey Experience
- Only in Edinburgh: What You Can Only Experience in

Edinburgh
- Staying Safe While on Holiday
- Recommended 3 Day Travel Itinerary

Thank you again for downloading the book and let's get started on exploring this beautiful city!

40

About Edinburgh: A Brief History and Background

Edinburgh lies at the Central Belt, right in between the Highlands and the Southern Uplands. It is the capital of Scotland and has been that since the 15th century. It is the seat of monarchy and houses the Scottish Parliament.

It is the second most populous city in the country and the 7th in all of the United Kingdom. With such a large population, it is easy to see how it could be a place of diverse activities.

The earliest settlement in Edinburgh can be traced as far back as the 15th century, but before that, it was a fort. However, archeological proof of earlier inhabitants shows that there were already people living in the area as early as the Mesolithic Era.

The volcanic plug, more popularly known as Castle Rock,

which sits in the middle of Edinburgh, served as a strategic and effective site for a fort. Rising an impressive 130 meters above sea level, it was a position that could easily be defended. When the English captured this part of Scotland in the 7th century, it was called Eiden's Burg. The term burg is an older word for fort and was added to "Eiden", which was what the area was called.

After serving as a fort, Edinburgh became home to Augustinian and Dominican Friars who both preached and helped commerce to improve. The town grew until it earned a chapter, which gave the residents certain rights. With its growing importance, the town once again fell under the English rule. The succeeding years witnessed the continuous warfare between England and Scotland with Edinburgh being caught in the middle.

By the 15th century, despite the continuous alternating invasions from Scotland and England, Edinburgh's population had grown to 15,000. The following centuries proved to be quite eventful with tragedies, such as the plague in the 17th and 19th centuries. There were also glorious occasions like the coronation of Charles I and the continuous improvement of the cityscape.

By the mid 19th century, Edinburgh had more than 170,000 residents. With the railway reaching the town and bridges built to provide more access, more and more immigrants made the Scottish town their new homes.

With such a long and rich history, Edinburgh has been home to distinguished experts in diverse fields, such as architecture, the arts, and sciences. Below are some of the famous folks who came from this town.

Alexander Graham Bell – Born in 1847, this Edinburgh native is the scientist, inventor, and engineer who has been credited in getting the patent for the first practical telephone.

Charles Darwin – Dubbed as the Father of Evolution, Darwin briefly called Edinburgh home when he attended the University of Edinburgh, which was then the best medical school in the United Kingdom. He stayed at the University from 1825-1827.

Sir Arthur Conan Doyle – This world famous literary writer was born in Edinburgh in 1859. He is the celebrated creator of Sherlock Holmes, a gifted detective with extraordinary sleuthing skills. With the popularity of his novels, this Edinburgh native is known to readers of all ages all over the world.

Sean Connery – Born in 1930, this Scottish actor has relished in the limelight. He was the first actor to portray the dashing British spy, James Bond, on the big screen. His other notable movies include Indian Jones, The Hunt for Red October and The Rock. His many awards and recognitions include the Kennedy Center Honors in 1999 and a knighthood in July of 2000 from Elizabeth II.

41

Geographical and Weather Information

Edinburgh lies on the Southern shore of the Firth of Forth, with the city center about 2 ½ miles from southwest of the Leith shoreline. The modern city is built on seven hills reminiscent of Rome's geography. The hills were products of ancient volcanic activity or intensive glaciations.

These hills are the following:
- Castle Rock
- Arthur's Seat
- Calton Hill
- Corstorphine Hill
- Craiglockhart Hill
- Braid Hill
- Blackford Hill

While the city is progressive with expansions regularly on the way, it is encircled by a green belt, which greatly affects the way it is developed. A green belt is an area protected from urban development to preserve it for natural wildlife. Expansions made in these areas must follow strict policies to ensure that these do not negatively affect the land. This is one of the many reasons why Edinburgh stayed lush despite being a cosmopolitan city.

Edinburgh is made up of different districts and areas, much like any other populated city. These areas retain the characteristics of the early settlements that were already in existence since the middle ages.

Residence types vary depending on the location. The ones

located in the central part of the city are buildings with multiple occupants who are commonly known as "tenements". Residences on the Southern and Western parts of the city are mostly detached or semi-detached villas as these areas have traditionally been the more affluent ones.

One other interesting part of Edinburgh is the Old and New Towns. UNESCO declared these areas as World Heritage Sites in 1955.

Edinburgh, much like the rest of Scotland, has a temperate maritime climate. This often comes as a surprise to most visitors, as it is not as cold as one usually expects from a city located that far north. Daytime winter temperature rarely falls below freezing point while summer months are also mild, not often exceeding 22 degrees Celsius.

Its location between the coast and the hills has earned the city the nickname the windy city. With winds coming from the southwestern and eastern direction, rain and fog have become the norm in Edinburgh.

42

The Best Time to Go: Holiday and Tourist Dates

With its mild and friendly climate, Edinburgh is a year-long destination, which both the locals and the foreign tourists can fully enjoy. However, to get a full experience of what the city has to offer, here are the best times to come and enjoy the local life.

Summer

This is undeniably the best time to be in Edinburgh. The months of June, July and August are full of activities and local events that are sure to give you a more memorable stay. With the warm, pleasant weather, you can enjoy the charming and vibrant city and experience the world's largest art festival.

The Edinburgh Festival runs from the end of July to the beginning of September. The Festival has about ten different events packed within the few weeks of summer. The following are just some of the most popular events included in the celebration:

Edinburgh Festival Fringe –

More locally referred to as the "Fringe", this festival is one of the events that draw crowds to this idyllic and cosmopolitan city. The festival's name may have been influenced by the fact that experimental and challenging performances are often included in the programs. These types of performances are often not invited to participate in more traditional art festivals.

In 2015, the Fringe lasted for 25 days with more than 50,000 performances and over 3,000 shows in 313 venues all over the capital.

The Fringe is an open-access festival, which means everyone can participate in the different categories including theater, comedy, opera, dance and a lot more. It is a festival, which helped build the careers of different artists and turned aspiring individuals into household names.

Edinburgh is a cultural haven during the Fringe, with events happening in various venues. Performances take place all over the city - from conventional halls and stadiums to the back of a taxi cab. By simply walking down the street, you can view art shows on sidewalks, watch a musical in the corner and perhaps listen to a band playing some awesome music for passers-by.

The different events range from paid performances to free ones where you simply donate what you please at the end of the show. The Fringe turns the city into a paradise for art lovers of all shapes and sizes.

Edinburgh International Festival –

This is an annual festival, which runs for three weeks in August. Performances for this one are strictly by invitation of the Festival Director. This gathers top performers in performance, music and other forms of art and serves to enrich the cultural life of Scotland, the UK, and Europe. The festival was first held after the Second World War as a way to bring back the arts into a war-torn Europe.

Edinburgh was chosen to host it as it fits the criteria organizers were looking for. They needed a city, which is capable of handling the large crowds that would be taking part or watching the performances. However, it had to be as picturesque as the cities that had previously hosted other similar festivals pre-war.

Other cities in the United Kingdom were considered before Edinburgh was eventually chosen. The festival performances are held in seven prominent venues located all over the city, including The Edinburgh Playhouse, Usher Hall, and Festival Theater. The 2016 festival included classical and contemporary performances of music, theater, dance, opera and workshops. Being in Edinburgh at the time of the festival will be a cultural experience that you will never forget.

Royal Edinburgh Military Tattoo –

A tattoo is a musical display or performance done by the military. This military tattoo is performed by the British Armed Forces, Commonwealth and other military bands. It is performed right in the heart of the city in front of the Edinburgh Castle.

The event draws thousands of people to Edinburgh to witness the spectacular performance. Two-thirds of the folks who come to see the tattoo are made up of local tourists with the rest coming from all over the world.

The popular military tattoo has sold out in advance for the past decade with people wanting to come and enjoy the musical performance done by the military personnel. To ensure that more folks get to enjoy the tattoo and hype up a little bit more excitement, the military bands also do free abridged performances in the Princes' Street Gardens. The musical performance is dubbed as "'Taste of the Tattoo."

The mini-show allows those who purchased tickets to the main performance to still enjoy the tattoo. In addition, it provides those who will be watching the Edinburgh Castle performance a preview of what the bands have in store for them.

Spectators are treated to a different side of the military with these entertaining musical performances of an artistic display of military precision.
Military Tattoo Website

Edinburgh International Book Festival or EIBF –
This event happens on the last three weeks of August and is held at the center of the Scottish capital at the Charlotte Square. It is the world's largest book festival, which draws book lovers of all ages from the four corners of the globe.

From the first time it was held in 1983, the book festival has brought to Edinburgh thousands of authors and publishers to share their love for literature with excited fans. Authors and personalities who have been a part of the festival include Margaret Atwood, Al Gore, Ian Rankin and Harry Potter creator, JK Rowling.

The EIBF is a festival designed for adults and kids alike. The Children's program runs alongside the general one and provides the youngsters with various activities, such as story-telling, workshops, and author events.

So if you or your traveling companions are book lovers, then this is the perfect time to spend a few weeks in the beautiful city.

International Edinburg Film Festival or EIFF –

First opening its gates in 1947, the EIFF is the oldest running film festival in the world. The event features a range of shows from full-length films to documentaries and music videos. It also recognizes top class entries with distinguished awards. These awards include the Michael Power award given by the jury and Audience Award going to crowd favorites.

The Edinburgh Filmhouse serves as the festival's home, with the featured films and videos shown in various venues all over the city. The EIFF segregate the entries into different categories that include, but are not limited to, animation, short films, and special screenings. So whatever genre you are interested in, you will find something to enjoy during the EIFF.

Autumn

With the festivals coming to an exciting close at the beginning of this season and the whole city turning a golden shade, Fall is a spectacular time to be roaming the streets of Edinburgh. There is still one more festival though that is an autumnal tradition, the International Storytelling Festival. So, if you are in town, then go ahead and check out the story telling events that are happening, featuring both traditional and contemporary.

Autumn is also when Bonfire Night happens. This amazing evening highlighted by an entertainment program and a half-hour fireworks show is also more popularly known locally as Guy Fawkes Night.

However, if you are more of a nature person, a walk around the city is a feast for your eyes. Edinburgh's 112 parks turn into a kaleidoscope of warm earth colors. The gorgeous palette of hues combined with the warm weather creates a relaxing environment. So, whether you go for a stroll down the historical streets or enjoy a cup of coffee in one of the local cafés, autumn in Edinburgh is a getaway worth taking.

Winter

The winter months in Edinburgh are truly a merry time. Christmas celebrations and Hogmanay draw hundreds of tourists to the city to take part in the festivities. In typical Edinburgh fashion, the celebrations last for weeks. The Christmas Season kicks off on November 18 and for six whole weeks, the entire city buzzes with excitement.

Kids of all ages will have a blast with the two ice skating rinks that are put up to help everybody get into the holiday spirit. What is winter after all if not for those afternoons spent gliding along the ice under a sprinkle of falling snow. So whether you and your family choose the ring-shaped rink St. Andrew's Square or the more traditional one Princes Street Gardens, you are guaranteed to have hours of fun and laughter.

One other thing that you and your traveling companions should certainly not miss is an afternoon spent exploring the Christmas Markets. This is perfect for you if you are looking for last minute gifts or souvenirs or just simply want to have the most Christmassy experience outside the North Pole. With fairy lights lining the street and the smell of bratwurst wafting from the shops, you will definitely find yourself humming a

Christmas carol as you stroll up and down the streets.

Being in town during the winter season also means you get a chance to be part of the Hogmanay celebrations. Hogmanay is the Scottish word used to refer to the last day of the year, so the celebration is literally a New Year's Eve party, but this one is by no means a simple one. The evening kicks off with streets bursting on the seams with revelers. Concerts and other performances are the norm as people wait for the highlight of the evening, which is, of course, the fireworks display at midnight.

You can choose to take part in the Torchlight Procession, which leads up to Calton Hill. It's remarkable finale of fire lighting, and fireworks are sure to be an experience you will remember for years to come.

Spring

This season is probably the quietest time to be in the city. If you are looking for a more relaxing holiday away from the crowds, then head on to Edinburgh during the months of spring. While not busy, the city is glorious at this time with the parks in vibrant colors from the flowers blooming in all their glory.

If you will be traveling with children, spring is also a good time to head on to the picturesque city. The International Science Festival and Imaginate Festival take place during this season.

The Edinburgh International Science Festival takes place either in March or April. It is a 2-week discovery of how science and technology can improve the way of life. It draws both adults and kids alike to the city, as they take part in a varied program including talks, exhibits and fun-filled family days.

The Imaginate Festival in Edinburgh happens towards the end of spring and is one dedicated to little kids. It features some of the best performances and theater and dance that are guaranteed to keep your little ones entertained.

Whatever season you decide to head on over to the Scottish capital, you will certainly find something to enjoy. This is perhaps the reason why thousands of tourists decide to enjoy holiday in the city, which fuses the excitement of city living with the enchantment of being close to nature.

269

43

The Top 5 Places to Stay at on a Budget

With so many things happening in Edinburgh all year round, one of the most challenging things you will probably experience is finding a place to stay. The great news is that there are different types of accommodations available all around the city.

While like any other capital city, it has its fair share of 5-star hotels and resorts it may not be the most cost-efficient way to enjoy your holiday. Other options available are budget hotels or holiday inns, contemporary hotels with warm Scottish ambiance and small elegant boutiques. This wide range of options means you can find what fits your budget without compromising comfort.

Here are some of the best places to stay at where you can get value for your money:

Rock House –

Nestled on the slopes of Calton Hill, this immaculate 18th-century house is one of the most recommended places to stay at when visiting Edinburgh. While only accessible by foot, it is only a few minute walk away from famous Princes Street. It is perfect for visitors who want to experience the city but who prefer to stay away from a conventional hotel setting.

Spectacular views of the city can be seen from virtually any part of the house. With delightfully remodeled rooms, the historic house offers comfortable amenities such as free Wi-Fi to keep you and your family happy. If you plan to stay for the day, then you can relax in the courtyard or walled gardens for an afternoon of peace and quiet.

One other appealing feature about the Rock House is its friendly prices. Room rates range from £60 - £150 a day with better prices offered for a longer stay.

Address:28 Calton Hill, Edinburgh EH7 5AA
Phone:0131 558 1108

Rock House Website

Old Waverly Hotel –

This is Edinburgh's oldest and most famous hotel located on Princes Street. The historical hotel is still one of the best accommodation options for visitors of the Scottish Capital. It is ideal for both tourists and corporate guests as it is close to the Financial District, as well as to some of the popular attractions in the city.

271

With affordable rooms that offer a spectacular view of the famous Princes Street, the Old Waverly Hotel remains a favorite all year round. The hotel also offers amazing deals, such as their winter £1 offer where guests only pay a pound per person per night. One other attraction that the hotel offers is it's in house restaurant "Cranston's Restaurant". The menu features local and traditional Scottish cuisine, which is an experience one should not miss when visiting Edinburgh.

Address:43 Princes St, Edinburgh
Phone:0131 556 4648

Old Waverly Hotel Website

Ten Hill Place Hotel –

This Eco-Friendly award winning hotel is located in Old Town, away from the main city traffic. However, it is still close to the Festival Theater and University of Edinburgh, which makes it a popular choice of tourists coming into the capital for the Edinburgh Festival. The hotel has a sophisticated ambiance, making it a preferred place to stay at for conferences or business trips.

Ten Hill Place has spacious rooms that offer good value for your money with complete amenities, such as WI-FI. It also boasts of friendly staff ready who are to help you out - from giving directions to the nearest Edinburgh attraction to ensuring you have a comfortable night. With affordable rooms and appealing packages offered, it is no wonder this hotel has gotten rave reviews from guests.

Address:10 Hill Pl, Edinburgh
Phone:0131 662 2080

Ten Hill Place Hotel Website

Brooks Hotel –

This newly refurbished boutique hotel located at the west end of the city center has been raking in great reviews from satisfied guests. The beautiful architecture and friendly ambiance has had a positive impact to those who chose to stay at the Brooks Hotel.

Located close to public transportation, the hotel has become a favorite stylish place to stay at for visitors who want to explore and experience the amazing Scottish capital. With prices ranging from £59 to £99, the spacious rooms with comfortable beds and power showers give you absolute value for your money.

Address:70-72 Grove St, Edinburgh
Phone:0131 228 2323

Brooks Hotel Website

Fountain Court Apartments-Morrison –
One other accommodation option that visitors to Edinburgh can choose are serviced apartments. These have grown quite popular in the last few years as more and more tourists opt to stay away from impersonal hotel rooms. They prefer their own spaces where it feels like home and they can prepare their

own meals if they want to.

Fountain Court Apartments offer this option at affordable prices. With prices ranging from £79 to £89, accommodations will certainly fit your budget. These pet friendly apartments also come with basic amenities, such as WI-FI access, kitchen and laundry facilities.

Address:228 Morrison St, Edinburgh
Phone:0131 622 6677

Fountain Court Apartments-Morrison Website

44

Getting Around: Edinburgh Transportation

Getting around the city is quite easy and manageable with attractions located close to each other. With other sites that are a bit further away, public transportation is available all throughout the city. Below are the different ways to get around the Scottish capital:

Trams –
Opened in 2014, the Tram line operates between the Airport and the city center. It passes through Princes Street, Haymart, Murrayfield Stadium, the Stenhouse Area and Gyle. Tram fees are the same as the Lothian bus fares. One other great thing about this public transportation is that you can use Lothian Day Tickets and Ridacards to pay for fare.

Phone:0131 475 0177
Tram Website

Edinburgh Airport Website

Edinburgh Airport Map
Phone:0844 448 8833

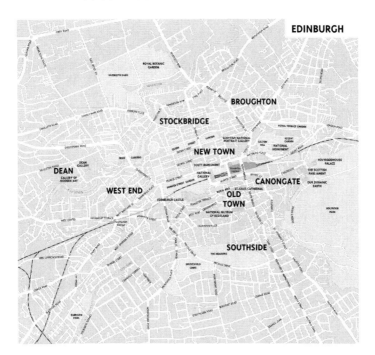

Buses –

This is the main form of transportation around the city. There are two major bus companies that operate in Edinburgh with a few smaller ones with fewer buses, but the main ones are the Lothian and First Bus. The latter has mostly buses that operate to and from outlying towns. So most of the buses you will see around the city are the dark red and white Lothian ones.

For convenience, you can purchase a Lothian Day Ticket for £4.00(£2.00 for kids) so you don't have to worry about getting the right change every single time. However, it is important to remember that you can only use these tickets on Lothian buses and not on the ones operated by other companies. If you plan to stay longer, then there are also other bus card options, such as the "Ridacard" and rechargeable "Citysmart" card.

Phone:0131 200 2323
Bus Website

Trains –

Getting across the city by train is the fastest and most efficient way to do it. However, with most of the top attractions close to each other around the city center, trains are not the best way to see everything that the place offers. There are five main lines in the city with all trains stopping at Waverly and Haymarket.

Phone:0344 811 0141
Train Website

If you are traveling to Edinburgh from London, you can take a train from Kings Cross station in London to Edinburgh.The journey is about four and a half hours.

London to Edinburgh Train Website

London to Edinburgh Train Website 2

London to Edinburgh Train Map

Kings Cross Station London Map

Car –

Armed with a map of the city or perhaps an app on your smartphone that can give you accurate directions on how to get to your destination, traveling by car may seem to be the perfect way to see the capital. However, with the city constantly in a hustle and bustle, finding a place to park may be an adventure on its own. To address this, the city has set up multi-level car parks where you can leave your cars and tour by bus instead.

Cycle –

If you want to see the city on two wheels, then the great news is that Edinburgh has cycle paths to make this possible. Safely segregated from the main traffic thoroughfare, the city's extensive network of paths makes cycling a great and green way to tour the Scottish capital.

Address:276 Leith Walk, Edinburgh
Phone:0131 467 7775
Cycle Rent Website

Cycle Rent Map

45

Famous Landmarks that you should not Miss

With two UNESCO World Heritage sites to offer plus dozens of other top attractions, Edinburgh is certainly a paradise for tourists. Hailed as the 'Athens of the North'', it boasts of scenic and historical landmarks that draw tourists from all over the world. Below are the top attractions that visitors to the lovely city should not miss.

Edinburgh Castle

This impressive Scottish landmark is perched atop of Castle Rock and has towered over the city since the 13th century. Undoubtedly, the castle is the country's most popular tourist attraction with over a million visitors per year. Its location on the peak means one can get a spectacular view of the city's other famous spots like Princes Street, the Royal Mile and the Palace of Holyroodhouse.

The landmark also offers a feature that every tourist looks for in a castle. The entrance is through a drawbridge over an old moat with bronze statues of Scottish heroes William Wallace and Robert the Bruce welcoming you as you enter.

Edinburgh Castle serves as the majestic backdrop to the Edinburgh Military Tattoo, which takes place every summer as part of the Edinburgh Festival.

Address:Castlehill, Edinburgh
 Phone:0131 225 9846
 Edinburgh Castle Website

 Edinburgh Castle Map

The castle is also known for the following:

The One O'clock Salute –
Located inside the castle is a distinctive curve walled section called the Half Moon Battery. On this wall is a time cannon, which is fired at 1pm from Monday to Friday.

What makes this tradition even more interesting is that while the cannon is being fired in the castle, a time ball is dropped at the Calton Hill Nelson Monument.

The Royal Palace – The palace was a witness to Scotland's colorful monarchy. In 1556, the ill-fated Mary, Queen of Scots, gave birth to the future King of England, James VI. The young prince assumed the Scottish throne on his first birthday and united England and Scotland in 1603. The last sovereign that stayed in the Royal Palace was Charles I when he spent the night there before his Scottish coronation in 1663.

Other attractions in the palace include The Great Hall, The Crown Jewels and the Stone of Destiny.

The Stone of Destiny is an ancient Scottish Monarchy symbol, which witnessed the coronations of Kings for centuries. The origin of the stone is wrapped in mystery, with the most famous legend being that it had been used by Jacob as a pillow when he dreamt of Jacob's ladder.

The Stone of Destiny used to be part of the King's throne in England until it was brought to Scotland in 1950. Nowadays, it sits in the throne room in the Royal Palace where you and other tourists can view it. The stone will leave Scotland again on the next coronation in Westminster Abbey.

St. Margaret's Chapel –

This private chapel, which used to be only for the Royals, is the oldest building in Edinburgh. It was built in the 11th century by David I and was dedicated to his mother, Queen Margaret, who was later canonized due to her many acts of charity. One interesting thing about the chapel is that it is maintained by the St. Margaret's Chapel Guild whose members are all named Margaret living in Scotland.

St. Margaret's Chapel Website

St. Margaret's Chapel Map

The Palace of Holyroodhouse and Holyrood Abbey

The Palace of Holyroodhouse is the Queen's royal residence when she is in Scotland, which draws thousands of visitors all year round. The Monarch stays at the palace during Holyrood

Week, which is usually at the end of June towards the beginning of July. And just like when she is in London, the Royal Standard of the United Kingdom is flown. The only difference is that it is the Scottish version that is used. Visitors to Edinburgh at that time are treated to a traditional parade including the Presentation of the Keys of the city of Edinburgh.

The spectacular and elegant palace has been at the center of Scottish history for centuries. It was the place where the coronation of James V and Charles I were held. It was also where James II and James IV were married.

The palace is open to the public when the Queen is not in residence, so visitors can tour the majestic Historic Apartments where Mary, Queen of Scots used to live. Another popular tourist attraction is the Historic Apartments with all its elegant furnishings, plasterwork, and tapestries.

Address:Canongate, Edinburgh

Phone:+44 131 556 5100

The Palace of Holyroodhouse Website

The Palace of Holyroodhouse Map

Royal Mile

The Royal Mile is the road that links Edinburgh Castle and the Palace Of Holyroodhouse. It is lined with historical landmarks and enchanting townhouses. Every Edinburgh visitor should make this road as one of the first stops with all the great shops including the traditional kilt makers, restaurants, and inns. The tall buildings on the street called "lands" can be as tall as 15-stories. The Royal Mile has narrow alleys with hidden backyards weaving in and around the "lands".

Tourists troop to the Royal Mile to see top attractions, like Castle Hill which is located at the upper end of the road. Some places that get quite a few visitors are the Camera Obscura and Outlook Tower. Your visit to the Royal Mile is also not complete if you do not drop by at the Tollbooth, with the city's tallest church towers and Lady Stair's Close where you can find the Writer's Museum.

Royal Mile Map

St. Giles Cathedral

Located on the Royal Mile right at the heart of the Old Town, Edinburgh's historic cathedral was consecrated in 1243.The church features remarkable medieval carvings and impressive stained glass windows, making it stand out from other religious landmarks in the city.

You can take a stroll around the church or join one of the guided tours that are available upon request. Admission is free, but you are invited to make a £3.00 donation per person. If you wish to capture the serene and beautiful surroundings, then you need to get permits for photography from the Information Desk.

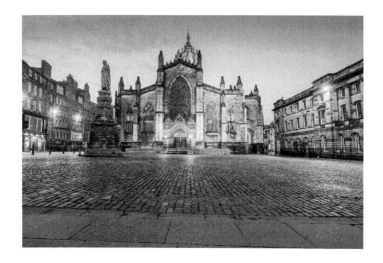

This attraction is located close to the rail station and is also accessible by bus.

Address:High St, Edinburgh

Phone:0131 225 9442

St. Giles Cathedral Website

St. Giles Cathedral Map

Princes Street

Located in one of the two UNESCO World Heritage sites, New Town, Princes Street is almost a mile long with enchanting gardens and sophisticated shops. A walk down this busy place will bring you to Jenners of Edinburgh, the oldest department store in the world. Other attractions that you can drop by include the grand House of Frasers on the western side and the quaint Princes Mall with its cozy shops and charming fountains.

While Princes Street is a shopper's paradise, it does have a lot more to offer. New Register House, the home of the Scottish National Archives is also an interesting place to visit. If you are interested in genealogy, then you will certainly have a grand time exploring the records on exhibit that go as far back as the 13th century.

One other place you should not miss visiting is the Princes Street Gardens, which is the home of the world's oldest floral clock. Visiting the gardens during winter is also a wonderful idea as you can spend an afternoon skating on the traditional outdoor rink.

Princes Street Website

Princes Street Map

Calton Hill

One of the seven hills the city is said to be built on, this attraction offers a unique and breathtaking view of the city that local and foreign tourists should definitely not miss. You can admire the majestic Edinburgh Castle and bustling Princes Street on the west and treat your eyes to the Old town on the South side. With its impressive altitude, you can even see as far as the docks at Leith from the peak of Calton Hill.

Also, not to be missed attractions on the Hill are the National Monument and Nelson Monument. The former was erected as a memorial to the casualties of the Napoleonic Wars. The memorial was designed after Parthenon in Athens, but was unfortunately unfinished due to lack of funding.

The Nelson Monument, which was unveiled in 1816, is where the cannonball is dropped at the same time the 1pm canon is fired at Edinburgh Castle.

Calton Hill Map

46

The Art Scene: Museums and Galleries to See

The Museum of Childhood

Located at the Royal Mile, this museum is a favorite among kids of all ages. It is the first museum, which is dedicated to displaying exhibits on the history of childhood. Its unique exhibits include games and toys, clothing, club memorabilia and other topics that cover the different generations and various stages of childhood.

A visit to the museum is more than just a day spent reminiscing your childhood days, as it also serves as an educational experience that you and your kids can share. From Barbie Dolls to pedal cars, the exhibits feature everything that brings you back to the innocent days of fun and play.

The Museum of Childhood is open seven days a week, and admission is free. Of course, donations are welcome to help with the upkeep of the museum. While it does not have its own café or restaurant, it is located right at the heart of The Royal Mile, and so it is close to a lot of exciting places for meals and refreshments.

Address:42 High St, Royal Mile, Edinburgh
Phone:0131 529 4142
The Museum of Childhood Website

The Museum of Childhood Map

Museum of Edinburgh

Located on Huntly House on the historic Royal Mile, the Museum of Edinburgh features exhibits that show the city's history and origin. From the medieval period to present day, the museum's collections are divided into two main categories – the Decorative and History. The Decorative collections include immaculate silver, creative pottery, and stunning Scottish glass.

The History part of the exhibits has archeological collections and ones that show the evolution of life in Edinburgh. From things found at home to popular past times of different generations, the Museum of Edinburgh has the most interesting items on display.

The museum is open from Mondays to Saturdays. During

the month of August, it is also open on Sundays. Admission is free with voluntary donations encouraged.

Address:142-146 Canongate, Edinburgh
Phone:0131 529 4143
Museum of Edinburgh Website

Museum of Edinburgh Map

Travelling Gallery

This unique art experience is a self-contained and mobile exhibit, which began in 1978. The first show was held in a double-decker that had been converted for the exhibit. The shows in the following years were so successful that by 1983, a custom built vehicle had been commissioned.

The Travelling Gallery features two shows a year, with each one running for an average of four months. It brings the exhibits closer to the public by staging it at different venues every day. It is something, which is certainly worth checking out when you are in the Scottish capital.

Because the gallery is mobile, it is highly recommended to contact the team in charge to find out where the show will be for the day you wish to go. Admission is free, so it is an adventure, which is culturally enriching without breaking your holiday budget.

Phone:0131 529 3930
e-mail: travellinggallery@edinburgh.gov.uk
Travelling Gallery Website

The Writer's Museum

Located in the Lady Stair's House on the Royal Mile, the Writer's Museum celebrates the three biggest names in Scottish literature. On the doorway at the entrance to the museum are words of warning that say "Fear the Lord and depart from evil", creating a mysterious air.

The three Scottish greats featured in the museum are Robert Burns, Sir Walter Scott, and Robert Louis Stevenson. Exhibits include portraits of Burns, the poet who wrote "Auld Lang Syne", personal items of Stevenson, the man responsible for novels such as Treasure Island, Kidnapped and the Curious Case of Dr. Jekyll and Mr. Hyde, and the printing press where

Scott's famous Waverly novels were printed on.

Scott is also known for his other works Ivanhoe and The Lady and the Lake.

Visitors like yourself will also have a grand time at the museum shop where you can get literary souvenirs to help you remember your museum experience.

Address:Lady Stair's House, Lady Stair's Close, Lawnmarket, Edinburgh
Phone:0131 529 4901
The Writer's Museum Website

The Writer's Museum Map

City Art Center

Art lovers of all ages will have a spectacular time at this six level gallery located near the Waverly Station. It features traditional and contemporary Scottish and Foreign art. The museum holds rolling exhibits that include photography, architecture and even Roman and Egyptian artifacts.

One of the most interesting exhibits featured in the gallery that had sci-fi and comic con fans going crazy was one of the Star Wars costumes.

Admission to the permanent exhibits is free with donations encouraged. Temporary shows, however, have admission fees.

2 Market St, Edinburgh
Phone:0131 529 3993
City Art Center Website

City Art Center Map

47

The Gastronomic Scene: Restaurants and Coffee Shops

Edinburgh is a gastronomic experience that any food lover will certainly enjoy. The Scottish capital has the most Michelin star restaurants in the country. You will find it absolutely delightful with different types of cuisine - from traditional Scottish to popular international favorites like pizza and burgers. Below are some of the restaurants and café's that locals and visitors recommend trying at least once.

Castle Terrace

The restaurant fuses local Scottish ingredients and elegant French style preparations. Castle Terrace is one of the most popular dining experiences in the city with reservations that you need to make months ahead. The good news is that you have a hundred percent assurance that the food and service will be worth the wait. You can be sure that the restaurant lives up to its reputation as a rising superstar in the culinary world.

In fact, this Old Town treasure only took 15 months to earn its first Michelin star.

The a la carte menu is updated per season, so their customers can take full advantage of ingredients that are locally available. With scrumptious dishes that include mouthwatering starters, delectable entrees, and sinful desserts, you can make sure that it is an experience worth spending money on.

Castle Terrace is also known for its impressive wine selection, which compliments the dishes served in the gastronomic haven.

Phone:0131 229 1222
Email:info@castleterracerestaurant.com
Castle Terrace Website

Castle Terrace Map

Oink Grassmarket

Located in Old Town's amazing Victoria Street is Oink Grassmarket. It is a restaurant, which specializes in hog roasts that are a treat for the senses. Even before getting to the restaurant, you can already smell the inviting aroma of roast as it wafts down the street.

Oink Grassmarket was set up by two farmers who turned moreish pork roast into a culinary dream. Served in three different sizes, the pulled pork dishes come with fluffy morning rolls, crackling and your sides including haggis and sage and onion stuffing. Soup of the day and cold drinks are also served to complete the meal. It is a filling dining experience that does not break the bank, with prices ranging from £2.95 for the Piglet size to the Grunter at £4.95

Address:34 Victoria St, Old Town, Edinburgh
Phone:07771 968233
Oink Grassmarket Website

Oink Grassmarket Map

The Witchery

This elegant restaurant offers the sophistication of fine dining without the uncomfortable, stiff environment. Located a stone's throw away from the Edinburg Castle, this Royal Mile treasure is nestled in a 16th-century building in the heart of Old Town. While it is a tad pricier than other restaurants, it does deliver the experience one expects from the amount you pay for.

It boasts an extensive wine list with around 800 selections, so you can find the perfect one to match your scrumptious meal. Patrons of this traditional restaurant recommend the lamb wellington for two or their signature steak tartare.

The prices while not cheap are still certainly affordable with a 3-course meal available at £36.00 and a 2-course lunch or theater supper for just £19.95

Address:Castlehill, The Royal Mile, Edinburgh
Phone:0131 225 5613
The Witchery Website

The Witchery Map

Nobles café, Bar and Restaurant

This popular food haunt is located on the Leith shore close to the scenic walkways. With its unique menu of Scottish ingredients and seafood like Haddock and Chips and Moules Frites, you will certainly be treated to a gastronomically delightful meal. Nobles also offer an impressive selection of ale from the tap and bottled.

Address:44a Constitution St, Edinburgh
Phone:0131 629 7215
Nobles café, Bar and Restaurant Website

Nobles café, Bar and Restaurant Map

First Coast

When on holiday in Edinburgh, the best places to eat are really the restaurants or bistros that locals frequent. With flavorful dishes at affordable prices, you get a taste of the city without breaking the bank. First Coast is certainly one of those places.

Located in Dalry Road, this award winning Bistro has been

a neighborhood favorite for the past decade. With a diverse menu that includes tasty seafood, meat, and vegetarian dishes, customers are treated to a unique dining experience.

First Coast uses local ingredients and fuses it with international flavors, such as Asian and Italian to create an unforgettable meal. The bistro also offers specials that change regularly to keep everything new and interesting. Bestsellers include Thai marinated chicken salad with cucumber, pepper and mango and ox cheek, polenta, parsnips & gremolata.

Prices are also pretty affordable at the elegantly decorated bistro. Ala carte meals range from £4.00 starters to £19.00 Angus Steak Entrée. You will also love the wine selections offered.

Address:97-101 Dalry Rd, Edinburgh
Phone:0131 313 4404
First Coast Website

First Coast Map

48

Edinburgh Night Life

Edinburgh, at night, is certainly as exciting and as adventurous as the unique attractions it offers. With the reputation as being the UK city with the most number of bars per capita, you are sure to find one, which is right up your alley. Here are a few recommended places to hang out in to have a memorable night.

Hector's

This charming and inviting place is everything you have ever imagined a Scottish Pub to be. With a relaxed ambiance and great ale that include local brews to international selections, Hector's is a local and tourist favorite. You can relax and enjoy a bit of conversation with the other patrons as you enjoy a relaxing Sunday evening sipping on beer or Bloody Marys and snacking on some delectable roasts.

Address:47-49 Deanhaugh St, Edinburgh
Phone:0131 343 1735

Hector's Website

Hector's Map

The Bongo Club

For some dancing and a night of music, the Bongo Club is one of the best places to head to. While it has been around for years, it used to have a nomadic life as it moved from venue to venue. The reason behind this was that there were no areas established as the best nightclub scene. However, in 2013, it found a permanent home. Now, it is literally an underground scene, located beneath the Central Library.

The club has become a popular place to unwind and let loose to the different types of music from reggae to soul that it offers. A quick visit to its website can fill you in on the events that will be happening, so you can check what is on during your stay in Edinburgh.

Address:66 Cowgate, Edinburgh
Phone:0131 558 8844
The Bongo Club Website

The Bongo Club Map

Sneaky Pete's

Located in Edinburgh's nightclub area at Cowgate, this

100-capacity club has featured gigs from up and coming as well as famous artists to promote the local music scene. The décor is street influenced with graffiti and murals adorning the seemingly dirty walls and dance floor; the club has a grungy ambiance that appeals to its patrons. If you are looking for some underground music and an evening spent experiencing Edinburgh's nightlife, then a visit to Sneaky Pete's is a must.

Be ready to dance and jam the night away with dozens of others on a crowded and vibrant dance floor. It is an evening that you will definitely not forget for a long time.

Address:73 Cowgate, Edinburgh
Phone:0131 225 1757
Sneaky Pete's Website

Sneaky Pete's Map

The Sheep Heid Inn

This historic pub located at the Causeway in Duddingston has been a favorite not just by the locals but by poets and past monarchs as well. Enchantingly restored, the Sheep Heid Inn is the oldest surviving watering hole in Edinburgh.

Nowadays, the pub's customers are mostly climbers or hikers of Arthur's Seat who are looking for a place to rest and relax before or after a strenuous day. The popular pub offers a taste of the country while still being in the city. The gastropub also offers a delectable treat to its hungry patrons.

Some of the foods included in the menu are BBQ Shredded Pork Sandwiches and Sausages and Mash. Prices are also reasonable with meals averaging about £8.00. The pub also has mid-week price specials, like a 3-course dinner with a bottle of wine included for only £22.00

Address:43-45 The Causeway, Edinburgh
Phone:0131 661 7974
The Sheep Heid Inn Website

The Sheep Heid Inn Map

The Electric Circus

Aptly named, this club can be practically anything one needs it to be. It is a part gig venue, part karaoke bar and part club. Located right behind the Waverly station, this incredible chameleon of a club has been the site for numerous colorful events, from up and coming bands showcasing their fresh music to hopefuls and wannabe's belting out to a chosen karaoke tune.

Patrons dance until the wee hours of the morning, celebrating the eccentric ambiance of the spot that has certainly and most definitely earned its name, circus.

You and your friends can immerse yourself in retro music, sing along with everybody as the red ball bounces across the screen or participate in fun workshops or classes like burlesque dance classes held in one of the rooms in the circus.

Address:36-39 Market St, Edinburgh
Phone:0131 226 4224
The Electric Circus Website

The Electric Circus Map

49

The Whisky Experience

There is one thing that you certainly cannot miss out on when you are in Edinburgh. You can't expect it to be a complete Scottish holiday unless you have some liquid gold or also more popularly known as Whisky. The best way to describe this drink is basically, Scotland in a glass. The Gaelic word for whiskey describes exactly how important it is to the locals.

Whisky, in Gaelic, is "uisge beatha", which means "the water of life", so make sure to enjoy a tour of any of the distilleries in and around the city. The best way to get started is to head off to the Scotch Whisky Experience on the Royal Mile.

The Scotch Whisky Experience has been introducing enthusiasts and beginners to the wonderful world of Scotch. It offers 1-day training school, enjoyable tastings and exciting tours.

In the training school, you spend the entire day learning

about whiskey. Most attendees are from the hospitality industry working to get certified. The course includes entertaining and educational hands-on activities, where you can even learn how to make your own drink at home. At the end of the session, you will get a certificate of expertise as proof that you had completed the course.

The next part of the experience is to book one of the available tours where you can explore nearby distilleries. These tours often include scotch tasting to help you better appreciate this Scottish traditional drink. The tour prices vary, ranging from £14.50 to £65.00 depending on what is included in the package.

There are also other Whisky tours that you can join that start in the city and lasts for a few days, continuing to the whiskey region of Scotland.

Address:354 Castlehill, Edinburgh
Phone:0131 220 0441
The Scotch Whisky Experience Website

The Scotch Whisky Experience Map

50

Only in Edinburgh: What you can Only Experience in the Scottish Capital

The Scots have always been proud and unique people and these local customs, traditions and specialties are best examples of just how amazingly different the city of Edinburgh is.

The Tartan Weaving Company

While it is common knowledge that the skirt looking clothing worn my Scotsmen are called kilt, not many people know
about the material that is used for it. Some people mistakenly
call it plaid, but the proper term is tartan. During your visit to
Edinburgh, you will find no shortage of this material. While
most of the ones for sale are of poor quality and created more
for tourists, there is a place where you can head off to and get
good tartan material.

Located at the end of the Royal Mile and just before the Castle
Esplanade is a non-descript building, which houses some of
the best kilt material in Edinburgh. It is called the Tartan
Weaving Company. It is the perfect place to get your material
for some serious kilting and learn about how the material is
made. The company offers displays of the history of tartan
making, as well as tours of the factory to give visitors a glimpse
of the process.

The Tartan Weaving Company Website

The Tartan Weaving Company Map

Unique Cuisine

If you have ever watched movies or documentaries about
Scotland, then there is a great chance that you already come
across some of the unique food offerings it has. While quite
interesting, some of these may need an acquired taste to fully
enjoy, but as they say, when in Rome! So, it would certainly
be a pity if you do not give a couple of these at least one try.

Haggis and Neeps – Traditionally served on Burns Night, this national dish has become famous worldwide because of the interesting assortment of filling that goes into the sausage. Haggis is made of innards and offal chopped up lungs, heart, and liver mixed with onions, suet, herbs and spices.

The filling is mixed together and stuffed into a skin bag made of a sheep's stomach. It is usually served with mashed potatoes and topped with a rich whisky sauce. While it may not sound appetizing, it does have an interesting taste and texture. Be sure to give it a try during your holiday at Edinburgh.

Address:Paisley Close, 105 High St, Edinburgh
Phone:0131 225 7064
The Royal McGregor Website (Hagis)

The Royal McGregor Map

Powsowdie – When called this, tasting the broth does not seem quite so adventurous. However, once you find out what it is also known as then it may seem like quite a daring task. Powsowdie is commonly known as Sheep's Head Broth. And yes, it really is made from sheep's head. The preparation may make some people cringe, but it is really quite rich and flavorful.

Rowan Jelly – While Jelly may not seem unique, this one is different from most fruit jellies that are either sweet or tart. Rowan berries are slightly bitter, making it a popular accompaniment to game or other rich tasting dish.

Scottish National Drink –

Edinburgh as the Scottish capital is a representation of Scotland's traditions and customs. One popular tradition is the country's national drink which is Whisky. As already discussed, there are quite a few distilleries around Edinburgh which is the reason why Whisky tours have become popular.

Address:197 High St, Edinburgh
Phone:+44 131 220 5277
The Albanach Website (Whiskey Bar)

The Albanach Map

Now, the unofficial national drink of Scotland is a carbonated beverage known as Irn Bru or Iron Brew. The bright orange colored drink has clever marketing techniques, which is the reason why it continues to rank over other internationally popular brands like Coca-Cola and Pepsi. It is a soft drink that you may want to give a try before leaving Edinburgh so you can experience exactly why locals love it so much.

51

Staying Safe While on Holiday

While the Scots are known to be warm and friendly, it is still wise to be aware of the best ways to stay safe while on holiday in Edinburgh. Here are some tips to keep in mind while you are in the safest city in the UK.

Take note of Emergency Numbers that you may need, such as local hospitals and police stations. The Emergency hotline in Edinburgh is **999**.

Some of the top attractions in Edinburgh are located in hilly areas. Wear comfortable shoes to prevent any accidents while walking around the city. In addition, be sure to bring necessities such as bottles of water, jackets, sunscreen and any other season appropriate things. The weather may get dry and warm or chilly on certain days, make sure you are prepared to deal with these conditions.

Watch out for tourist traps. Edinburgh is a popular tourist

destination that draws people from all over the world. With so many folks coming to town, the tourist trade is certainly on the up and up. So be careful when shopping for souvenirs as most of these may be overpriced and not of good quality.

If you are planning to take the bus around the city, make sure you have plenty of change to avoid any inconvenience. Bus drivers will rarely split your money if you do not have the exact amount so you may end up losing money over bus rides. You can also opt to get the day tickets so you no longer have to worry about getting the right change when getting on the buses.

Check up with local law enforcement or tourism offices about the places to avoid. While Edinburgh is generally a safe city to explore, tourists are advised to stay away from the Wester Hailes in the southwest and the housing estates of Pilton and Muirhouse as these areas are known to have a high crime rate and drug abuse.

Scotland Police Website

Emergency Number - 999

52

Recommended 3-day Travel Itinerary

With so much to offer, it seems almost impossible to fit in all the sites and sounds that Edinburgh has to offer in just 72 hours. However, with the right plan, you can fully experience the city in three days whatever time of the year you go. Below is a recommended travel itinerary for you and your family.

However, before we start on the different landmarks and attractions you can visit, the first step is to find a centrally located place to stay. The great news is that as discussed in a previous chapter, there are various types of accommodations in and around the city center that will surely fit your budget. If you are traveling with family or friends, you can choose a serviced apartment or boutique hotel to stretch your budget.

Day 1 – Edinburgh Castle, Royal Mile and the Palace of Holyroodhouse

You can spend your first day exploring the most popular attractions of Edinburgh. Edinburgh Castle and Holyroodhouse are connected by the Royal Mile, so you can explore it without the need to travel in circles.

Start with the majestic Edinburgh Castle at Castle Rock Hill and explore the fort that started it all. Aside from the different sites inside the castle like the Royal Palace and St. Margaret's Chapel, you can also enjoy your first bird's eye view of the city.

Edinburgh Castle Map

After getting a fill of the Castle, you can head on to the Royal Mile and immerse in the beautiful buildings and picturesque winding alleys. The road is lined with charming cafes and stores that offer a taste of the Scottish capital. The Royal Mile is also home to quite a few interesting museums that you may want to pop into and explore. Most of these do not charge an admission fee and only ask for minimal donations.

Royal Mile Map

Just a few minutes down the road is the Queen's official residence in Scotland, the Palace of Holyroodhouse. If you are in town around the end of June, then you can get a glimpse of the Scottish version of the Royal Standard being flown.

Holyroodhouse Map

The Palace has sections that you can tour, so be sure to sign up for that so you can see the elegant furnishings and beautiful works of art on display.

Day 2 – New Town and Leith

After a hearty and filling Scottish breakfast, your second day will be, once again, a treat for all senses. Spend the day exploring the sites of New Town. The area is full of shops where you can start filling up on souvenirs to remember your trip by. Whether you choose a tartan or some other colorful and clever knickknack, have fun exploring what the stores have to offer.

Word Of Mouth Website (Breakfast Recommendation)

Word Of Mouth Map

Address:3A Albert St, Edinburgh
Phone:+44 131 554 4344

Princes Street in New Town also has a lot of gastronomical delights, so you can take a quick break for lunch while also admiring the beautiful parks in the area. Before leaving the street, make sure to head to the Gardens and take loads of pictures for your Instagram and other social media accounts.

Princes Street Map

Afterward, you can go to Leith where you can stop by the Royal Yacht Brittania. This floating museum is ranked as the 3rd must see attractions in Edinburgh. This historical Royal floating palace is a treat to explore. With rooms and decks included in the audio guided tour, you and the rest of your group can have a glimpse of the Royal Family's official yacht.

Address:Ocean Terminal, Ocean Dr, Edinburgh
Phone:0131 555 5566
Royal Yacht Brittania Website

Royal Yacht Brittania Map

If you want to do some more shopping then you can have your fill at the Ocean Terminal, or you can simply relax in one of the many cafes and restaurants inside the shopping complex to recharge before your next adventure.

While you are in Leith, be sure to take a leisure stroll down the paths of the Water of Leith Walkway. If you have bicycles rented for the day, it also makes for a good biking path. The area is an interesting palette of colors with the water and surrounding foliage.

Water of Leith Walkway Website

Water of Leith Walkway Map

Day 3 – Calton Hill, Arthur's Seat and the Roslyn Chapel

Your last day in the city is by no means any different from the previous days. It is still full of adventure and excitement as you continue to explore what the city has to offer.

If you want a bird's eye view of the city on your final day, you can choose between Arthur's Seat and Calton Hill. While both are spectacular locations, the former is a bit more strenuous. Pick which of those two peaks will fit your hiking skills.

Arthur's Seat Map

Calton Hill Map

There are also still quite a few galleries, museums, parks and castles that you can explore, so simply pick out the ones that capture your interest, as well as the rest of your party. The bus lines in the city are dependable so you should have no problem getting about. Check out the Writer's Museum to learn more about the greatest Scottish writers responsible for literary works such as Dr. Jekyll and Mr. Hyde.

Writer's Museum Map

You can visit the Museum of Childhood to view interesting exhibits that feature items from the different stages of growing up. From doll houses to spinning tops, it is a great way to reminisce about your childhood and learn about previous generations.

Museum of Childhood Map

One destination that you cannot leave without seeing, especially if you are a Dan Brown fan is the Roslyn Chapel. This chapel was made famous in the novel "The Da Vinci Code". As a result, it has drawn more and more visitors to this unique church, which combines different architectural elements.

Roslyn Chapel Map

Roslyn Chapel Website

Address:Chapel Loan, Roslin
Phone:+44 131 440 2159

For Guided Tours In Edinburgh CLICK HERE

53

Conclusion

Whether you are traveling with friends or family, Edinburgh has a lot to offer. With its numerous historical landmarks, picturesque views and exciting festivals that are happening almost the whole year round, it is no surprise that it continues to attract tourists from all over the world.

A city that fuses busy urban lifestyle with the laidback and relaxed ambiance of country living, Edinburgh is an ideal spot for whatever holiday you may have in mind.

From romantic getaways to adventures with friends and family, you can be sure that you will find something to satisfy your senses in the Scottish capital.

Thank you again for downloading the book! I hope you were able to get the information you need to enjoy your trip to Edinburgh.

If you received value from this book, I want to ask you for a favour. Would you be kind enough to leave a review for this book on Amazon?

http://goninjatraveler.com/books/

information herein, either directly or indirectly.

Respective authors own all copyrights not held by the publisher.

The information herein is offered for informational purposes solely, and is universal as so. The presentation of the information is without contract or any type of guarantee assurance.

The trademarks that are used are without any consent, and the publication of the trademark is without permission or backing by the trademark owner. All trademarks and brands within this book are for clarifying purposes only and are the owned by the owners themselves, not affiliated with this document.